M000248168
INCLUDING
STUDENTS WITH
Disabilities
IN ADVANCED
SCIENCE CLASSES

INCLUDING STUDENTS WITH *Disabilities* IN ADVANCED SCIENCE CLASSES

LORI A. HOWARD
ELIZABETH A. POTTS

Arlington, Virginia

Claire Reinburg, Director
Jennifer Horak, Managing Editor
Andrew Cooke, Senior Editor
Wendy Rubin, Associate Editor
Amy America, Book Acquisitions Coordinator

ART AND DESIGN
Will Thomas Jr., Director
Rashad Muhammad, Graphic Designer

PRINTING AND PRODUCTION
Catherine Lorrain, Director

NATIONAL SCIENCE TEACHERS ASSOCIATION
David L. Evans, Executive Director
David Beacom, Publisher

1840 Wilson Blvd., Arlington, VA 22201
www.nsta.org/store
For customer service inquiries, please call 800-277-5300.

16 15 14 13   4 3 2 1

NSTA is committed to publishing material that promotes the best in inquiry-based science education. However, conditions of actual use may vary, and the safety procedures and practices described in this book are intended to serve only as a guide. Additional precautionary measures may be required. NSTA and the authors do not warrant or represent that the procedures and practices in this book meet any safety code or standard of federal, state, or local regulations. NSTA and the authors disclaim any liability for personal injury or damage to property arising out of or relating to the use of this book, including any of the recommendations, instructions, or materials contained therein.

Library of Congress Cataloging-in-Publication Data
Howard, Lori A., 1961-
Including students with disabilities in advanced science classes / by Lori A. Howard and Elizabeth A. Potts.
pages cm
Includes bibliographical references and index.
ISBN 978-1-936959-27-3 — ISBN 978-1-938946-93-6 (e-book) 1. Science--Study and teaching—United States. 2. Children with disabilities—Education—United States. 3. Children with disabilities—Education—Law and legislation—United States. I. Potts, Elizabeth A. II. Title.
Q181.H695 2013
371.9--dc23

2012050313

CONTENTS

ABOUT THE AUTHORS

Lori A. Howard, PhD, is an assistant professor of special education at Marshall University in West Virginia. She has taught a variety of special education courses. She has written and presented at conferences on the topics of inclusion, co-teaching, students with disabilities in science, and including students with disabilities in advanced placement courses.

She has also co-written books on co-teaching, including *Team Teaching Science: Success for All Learners*. She and Beth Potts have previously written *How to Co-Teach: A Guide for General and Special Educators*.

Elizabeth A. Potts, PhD, is the director of Special Education Programs and an assistant professor at the University of Virginia's Northern Virginia Center. She has written and presented at conferences on the topics of inclusion, co-teaching, data collection, and evidence-based practices.

INTRODUCTION

Why This Book

Life is either a daring adventure or nothing.
—Helen Keller

Currently, more and more students with disabilities are choosing to take accelerated high school science classes such as Advanced Placement (AP), International Baccalaureate (IB), or honors classes (Bleske-Resech, Lubinski, and Benbow 2004). Concurrently, there has been an increased focus on science, technology, engineering, and math (STEM) courses in the media, from the U.S. Department of Education, and in professional development course offerings. As the push continues to increase the number of students who take accelerated courses in science, it is likely that more students with disabilities will be encouraged to take these courses or will be placed in advanced courses as a matter of school culture (e.g., everyone takes honors courses).

Often the teachers of accelerated and honors classes are experienced and knowledgeable about science. In many cases, they have earned an advanced degree in a science-related field; however, they may have little or no experience with special education or "including" students with disabilities in these classes. Advanced or accelerated courses are not usually team taught with a special education teacher (Linz, Heater, and Howard 2011). Consequently, science teachers may lack ready access to special educators to share strategies with them to foster the success of students with disabilities in these courses and independent knowledge of those specific strategies.

Although these are high school courses, they are often taught as university-level courses. Many of the students in these classes are high achievers academically with very compliant classroom behavior. Due to the content of the discipline (e.g., physics, chemistry) and the nature of the students, expectations for *all* students in such classes are typically higher than for students in standard classes. Many students with disabilities can succeed in this classroom environment (Hallahan, Kauffman, and Pullen 2009); however, both the science teacher and the students with disabilities will benefit from specialized knowledge of instructional strate-

INTRODUCTION

gies, special education requirements, classroom behavioral interventions, and an understanding of how to apply individualized education program (IEP) accommodations in the accelerated or advanced science classroom. A bonus is that many of these accommodations will benefit students without disabilities as well.

The purpose of this book is to provide the reader (you) with information and guidance on how to successfully include students with disabilities in your accelerated science classroom. Many of you have successfully taught these science classes for years and do not need assistance on the content of science or how to teach. This book will specifically focus on classroom success for students with disabilities. It will also provide practical guidance for situations that may occur in your classes.

The beginning of the book will provide an overview of special education terminology and law as background for working with the IEP team. Several research- or evidenced-based strategies for use in the classroom will also be discussed, as will suggestions for dealing with difficult classroom behavior and management issues. Although the research base for most of these suggestions centers around use in classrooms other than advanced science classes, there is evidence to generalize the strategies for use with multiple populations, so it is logical to extend their use to students in your advanced science classes. We will give special attention to the unique requirements of advanced and accelerated classes such as laboratory experiments, field trips, and high-stakes testing (e.g., College Board testing).

One of our assumptions in this book is that students with disabilities in accelerated and honors classes are on a path to college. An essential skill set for success in postsecondary education is a student's knowledge of him- or herself, paired with the ability to set and work toward goals and to speak up for him- or herself to get the resources needed to meet those goals. Many students pick up these self-advocacy skills without direct prompting and instruction, but students with disabilities need opportunities to develop their self-advocacy skills to help ensure success in a college environment. All of the students' teachers need to be aware of the skills and prompt the student to practice the skills at every opportunity. Throughout this book, you will find special boxes called "Fostering Student Independence." These boxes, written in language directed at students, will provide you with ideas and bullet points to help students think about and advocate effectively for their own needs. See Chapter 2 for more about self-advocacy and "Fostering Student Independence" on the next page for an example of this student-centered box.

Some science teachers may have an understandable reluctance to include students with physical or behavioral challenges in their classes. These teachers may fear that one student will disrupt the classroom environment for all of the learners or that one student may require too much individual instruction, thus reducing time for others. These concerns can be addressed through learning more about particular disabilities and strategies to use to foster success. After all, students

INTRODUCTION

FOSTERING STUDENT INDEPENDENCE

Most teenagers want more independence and control over their own destiny, but this requires a set of skills that you may not have perfected yet. These "Fostering Student Independence" text boxes are designed to help you understand and develop the skills you need to be more in control of your academic life.

with disabilities cannot be excluded from these classes just because they have a disability (U.S. Department of Education 2004).

In fact, students with disabilities can also have special talents or gifts; these students are often referred to as *twice exceptional* (Hallahan, Kauffman, and Pullen 2009). These gifted and talented students can excel in advanced classes when learning supports are in place. Consider the "chemistry whiz" who needs an outline to write up the lab report. The student is terrific at solving problems, balancing chemical equations, and doing the experiment, but she needs help organizing her writing. Once an advanced organizer (outline) is provided, she can write up the lab report. So, with a small adaptation or accommodation, the student can successfully participate in the advanced or accelerated classroom.

Another purpose of this book is to encourage science teachers to embrace including students with disabilities. Some great scientists had their own challenges to overcome on their way to greatness. Albert Einstein was considered slow in school. Despite his lack of promise during his elementary years, he certainly became adept at science. This is just one example, and not every student with a disability will become the next Einstein; however, there may be some very good scientists waiting for the opportunity that your accelerated class offers. It is our hope that you, the science teacher, will become familiar with the context of special education. It is also our belief that in working to provide the learning supports and accommodations needed for students with disabilities to be successful, you will benefit all of your students and your own growth as a teacher will be enhanced. You will find new and creative ways to manage lab experiments so that all of the students will benefit, you will think of new ways to design your instruction with individual needs in mind, you will overcome fears related to behavioral flare-ups in your classroom, and you will be more confident in working with your special education counterparts and the IEP team.

To help you make practical connections, each chapter contains a checklist called "Ideas to Get You Started" that creates action items based on the chapter content. We encourage you to consider different ways in which to support the concepts you are teaching and the ways in which you structure your classroom. As you become more comfortable making classroom accommodations for students with disabilities, we also hope that you come to recognize and appreciate your unique gifts as a teacher.

References

Bleske-Resech, A., D. Lubinski, and C. P. Benbow. 2004. Meeting the educational needs of special populations: Advanced Placement's role in developing exceptional human capital. *Psychological Science* 15 (4): 217–224.

Hallahan, D. P., J. M. Kauffman, and P. C. Pullen. 2009. *Exceptional learners: An introduction to special education.* 11th ed. New York: Allyn & Bacon, Pearson Education.

Linz, E., M. J. Heater, and L. A. Howard. 2011. *Team teaching science: Success for all learners*. Arlington, VA: NSTA Press.

U.S. Department of Education. 2004. Individuals With Disabilities Education Act. *http://idea.ed.gov*

CHAPTER 1

Basic Special Education Terms and Laws

We know what you're thinking: "I'm not a special educator, so why are these terms and laws important to me?" As a science teacher, you will not be responsible for knowing the intricacies of disabilities and disability laws, but the fact that you will have students with disabilities in your classroom means that you do need to have at least a working knowledge of disability terminology and laws. Sharing a common vocabulary with the special educators working with your students with disabilities will enable you to have more meaningful conversations about how to serve students and participate more actively in individualized education program (IEP) meetings (Hallahan, Kauffman, and Pullen 2012; see the "IEP" section later in this chapter and Chapter 2 for more information).

Additionally, having background knowledge about the laws will give you a context for why certain features, such as testing accommodations, are required and how the team of individuals working with the student comes to the decision about what is necessary. Though you do not need to be an expert, some understanding of basic concepts will allow you to be an active participant in discussions related to your students with disabilities. Understanding these concepts will allow you to apply your science background to the special education context instead of spending time and energy trying to figure out what everyone is talking about.

Laws and Terms

If you will be teaching a student with a disability, it is important to understand some terms and basics of the law as they pertain to a student's work in your class. The first federal law that mandated that schools identify and serve students with disabilities, the Education for All Handicapped Children Act, was passed in 1975 (Hallahan, Kauffman, and Pullen 2012). The law has been renewed and updated a number of times since 1975, most recently in 2004, and is now referred to as the Individuals With Disabilities Education Act, or IDEA.

CHAPTER 1

The basic premise of special education law is that all students with disabilities must be provided with a *free appropriate public education* in their *least restrictive environment*. What that means in practical terms is that public schools must provide for—and cannot deny access to—the education of all children with disabilities. An appropriate education implies, and case law has further defined, that the school works to provide access to the general education curriculum, accommodating the disability such that the student can perform and learn as much like his or her peers as possible. Schools are to provide services (education) to the child in his or her least restrictive environment, in the setting in which he or she can best thrive, while spending as much time as possible with his or her nondisabled peers (Hallahan, Kauffman, and Pullen 2012).

This means that when you have a child with a disability in your advanced science classroom, the IEP team (see the IEP section in this chapter) has decided the student can be successful in your classroom, often with some accommodation. Many people incorrectly interpret *least-restrictive environment* to mean that the student should always receive services in the general education classroom, but the law is clear that the general education classroom is not the most appropriate placement for all students. Even though your accelerated courses are more cognitively demanding than the typical science class, the students with disabilities who gravitate toward your class will be able to succeed if given a little support and understanding from you.

Another law you should be familiar with is Section 504 of the Vocational Rehabilitation Act. Commonly referred to simply as 504, this law provides in all public schools, extending to colleges and universities and not just K–12, a guarantee of access to school and curriculum. This may sound exactly like the protection provided by IDEA, but the two laws define *disability* differently and require different levels of accommodation.

For instance, if a student with a disability qualifies for IDEA, they require special education, or specialized instruction designed to meet their needs and described in the IEP, because the disability has an educational impact (Kauffman and Hallahan 2005). In your classroom, that may look like adjustments to the amount of material for which a student is responsible or a change in the method of assessing the student's in-class work. Conversely, a child who does not meet the definition of disability under IDEA but meets the definition under 504 could not receive the above accommodation (see Figure 1.1 for a definition). Accommodations under 504 should be limited to those that provide comparable access to education as is experienced by peers without disabilities (deBettencourt 2002). For example, a student may qualify for a 504 plan if they have a temporary disability, such as a broken arm, and need accommodations related to the physical act of writing. An IEP is only developed if a student qualifies for special education.

FIGURE 1.1. ACCOMMODATIONS AND MODIFICATIONS

Part of the specialized instruction that is the core of special education is providing accommodations and modifications to the general education curriculum to allow students with disabilities to succeed. *Accommodations* include changes to how students access the curriculum, or produce responses to assessment of that curriculum, with the idea that the students will be able to learn and perform without being hindered by the disability (Edgemon, Jablonski, and Lloyd 2006).

A *modification* includes a change to the curriculum for which the student is responsible. Students who will be in your advanced science classes will be those who need accommodations.These students are capable of and should be held to the same standards as their nondisabled peers, but they may require some alterations to the presentation of material, the format in which they produce information for assessment, or the amount of time they need to complete certain tasks. Conversely, students who require modifications (and will not be placed in your class) will not have mastered the building blocks of the content, thus requiring an alteration to the curricula.

An additional difference is who, at the school level, is in charge of the process. For special education, under IDEA, a special educator tends to be the student's case manager and leads the process; for 504 plans, each school has a 504 compliance officer or coordinator who will guide the process, but this should not be someone from the special education department. If you have students with 504 plans in your advanced science class, the 504 coordinator should provide you with the plan, which contains little more than accommodations, and you should direct all questions to the school's 504 coordinator or compliance officer.

It is important you understand that these are two different laws, with two different sets of rules, so that if you have students who qualify for both situations, you will understand why they may receive different accommodations, even if you think they may both benefit from the same adjustments in instruction.

FOSTERING STUDENT INDEPENDENCE

Student, as you get older, it becomes more important for you to become familiar with the laws that ensure that you, as an individual with a disability, have rights. IDEA defines the right you have to an education, one that is appropriate for you given your disability. As you move on to college and the working world, you will need to be familiar with Section 504 and the Americans With Disabilities Act because these laws will protect your rights for the rest of your life. You have the right to an education, you have the right to be evaluated for a job as if you do not have a disability, and you have the right to appropriate accommodations in both college and the workplace. You have to know the law to be sure that your rights are not being violated.

CHAPTER 1

IEP

When a student with a disability needs special education, a team of people gather to write an individualized education program (IEP) that outlines the educational plan for that student. This group of people is called the IEP team and consists of, at a minimum, the student (the law says "when appropriate," but it will always be appropriate to include your upper-grade students who are working on advanced material), a special educator, a general educator, the parents, and an administrator. If the student has needs in other areas—such as occupational, physical, or speech therapy—other professionals may be part of the team as well. The primary purpose of the IEP team is to write an IEP, the legal document that guides the student's instructional and school day (Bateman and Linden 2006). See Chapter 2 for more information about working with the IEP team.

The IEP is a good document for you to understand. It can provide you with background information about the student and his strengths and weaknesses, and it may also give you valuable information about what will help the student succeed (e.g., the student responds well to positive feedback or the student works well in groups with high levels of structure). For students who are 16 years and older, the IEP also contains important information about preparing the student for the transition from high school to the next phase in life. Most of the students in your advanced classes are preparing for college. As a valued member of the IEP team, you can help the team consider what the student needs to do in preparation for postsecondary success. We discuss this preparation more thoroughly in Chapter 2.

Even if there is no special educator sharing your classroom with you, and even if you are not actively involved in writing the IEP, you are still legally responsible for following the plan laid out in the IEP. We do encourage you to be an active member of the IEP team, especially the year before the student enters your classroom. Who has better knowledge of the demands of your classroom than you? The IEP will take the form of goals, or skills and tasks, that the student is working to learn or improve, accommodations and modifications the student needs to be able to access the general education curriculum, and statements of how much time and in what way students will receive specialized services to meet their goals (Bateman and Linden 2006). The key parts that you will want to be familiar with are outlined below, with exception of the transition plan, which is detailed in Chapter 2.

Present Level of Performance

The IEP contains a description of the student's present level of academic achievement and functional performance, often shortened to *present level of performance* or PLOP. A well-written PLOP contains a snapshot of the student, both behaviorally and academically. Reading the PLOP should give you an idea about the student's areas of strength, weakness, and interest. Knowing a student's strengths and interests can help you connect to the student and set the student up for success if he or she struggles early in the school year. Maybe organization is an area of strength, so you may assign the student to organize classwide data in an early class activity to boost self-esteem and reinforce the idea that the student can succeed in your classroom. Additionally, the PLOP will often contain references to methods and systems that have helped the student succeed; having this information early in the school year will allow for a more seamless transition into your classroom. For instance, if a student works better in very small groups, that may be reflected in the PLOP and may be something you can accommodate in your class activities.

Measurable Goals

Weaknesses reflected in the PLOP will often be reflected again in the goals section of the IEP, because there will be a goal associated with improving the weakness. This can include academics (such as reading level), behaviors (such as raising hands), and even study skills (such as turning in homework). Students in your advanced-level science classes are more likely to have goals related to behavior and study skills than academics. Your role in goals is likely to be minimal. The special education case manager should discuss any goals that the student will be working on in your classroom, what (if anything) you should do to address those goals, and how to provide data related to student progress toward IEP goals. We will discuss this communication more in Chapter 2.

Accommodations

Accommodations also extend from the weaknesses described in a student's PLOP. We defined accommodations earlier in this chapter. Accommodations are essentially adjustments you make to your instruction, or the student's interaction with your instruction, so the student can perform in the classroom as if he or she did not have a disability (Edgemon, Jablonski, and Lloyd 2006). This does not mean you have to change content or lower your standards for students with disabilities; we put accommodations in place to provide *access* to instructional content or *access* for students to demonstrate their knowledge and understanding of that content. Accommodations should match each individual student's needs, based on what he or she needs to succeed in your science class. Table 1.1 (p. 6) provides some examples of common accommodations and rationales for why IEP teams may determine certain accommodations are necessary for a specific student. Note that some accommodations are changes you can make to your instruction as a basic change in practice—they will benefit students with or without disabilities and will not make the students who need the adjustment stand out from the rest of the students. This aligns with the idea of universal design for learning. See Figure 1.2 (p. 7) for more information.

TABLE 1.1. EXAMPLES OF COMMON ACCOMMODATIONS

Student Need	Course Requirement	Accommodation	Why the Accommodation Is Appropriate
Bill's learning disability affects his memory and his ability to memorize and recall facts.	Students must memorize certain chemical elements and their atomic numbers and weights.	Bill uses a periodic table of elements for all activities.	Using a table allows Bill to demonstrate his ability to use the information on the periodic table while accommodating his disability in memorization.
Sarah's past surgeries for a chronic other health impairment (OHI) caused her to have a latex allergy.	Students dissect fetal pigs that have been injected with latex to highlight specific features.	The school purchases pigs without latex, or Sarah completes a fetal pig dissection on a computer.	Sarah is still able to experience the objectives related to the dissection without being exposed to the potentially fatal allergen.
Joe has obsessive compulsive disorder and tends to focus on only doing things if they are perfect.	Students complete a physics lab.	Provide step-by-step directions in writing so Joe has a reference for the tasks at hand, encouraging him to mark off (or erase) each step as it is completed.	Joe can successfully complete the same lab as his peers, with supports in place to help him focus on the lab instead of each individual component.
Elsie's anxiety impairs her ability to do oral presentations.	Students present a science fair project.	Elsie can record her presentation and show a video instead of doing a live presentation.	Elsie will demonstrate her understanding of the material in an environment not affected by her disability.
Francie's learning disability affects her writing, specifically spelling and editing.	Students write a lab report. Students also answer an essay question on a test, requiring them to explain how something works.	Francie can take her lab report home to finish it, providing her with more time and less pressure to edit her work. On tests, Francie will not be docked for writing format or grammar.	These accommodations allow Francie to demonstrate mastery of the content without be impeded by her writing disability.

FIGURE 1.2. UNIVERSAL DESIGN FOR LEARNING (UDL)

UDL is centered around the idea that if we design instruction to meet the needs of most students, instead of thinking only about those who require no special consideration, we will need to make fewer accommodations and changes for students who may have special needs. The most classic universal design example is adding wheelchair ramps in new construction—designing something that more people can use allows people who have physical disabilities, push strollers, and use walkers, as well as able-bodied individuals, to all use a building without any accommodation (CAST 2010). Chapter 4 will discuss ways UDL can manifest in your advanced science classroom.

As a member of the IEP team, you will have an opportunity to help determine appropriate accommodations, and it is important for you to be involved since you are the expert on the cognitive, physical, and social demands of your classroom. An appropriate accommodation provides the student with access to the curriculum without giving them an advantage over their peers (Edgemon, Jablonski, and Lloyd 2006). When considering an accommodation, ask this question: If every student had this opportunity, would it greatly improve the performance of those without disabilities? In general, the answer should be no. The accommodation is like an ankle brace for an athlete with a hurt ankle—if all athletes wore ankle braces, those without injuries would not perform better, but the athlete with an ankle injury will perform as if he does not have the injury (or at least as if the injury were not as bad). Likewise, a good accommodation would not greatly improve the performance of a student without a disability, but will allow the student with a disability to perform as if he or she did not have the disability (Fuchs et al. 2000).

Be creative in thinking about ways to accommodate a student's disability. Consider ways to provide accommodations without singling the student out. For instance, why not provide step-by-step directions for everyone? Instead of giving only oral directions, writing the directions on the board will benefit students with and without disabilities and will also give your voice a break! If students are anxious about speaking in class, provide other ways for them to demonstrate understanding—maybe give everyone an exit slip with key points from the day. With careful planning, you can incorporate accommodations seamlessly into your classroom without changing the integrity of your instruction or assessment.

Also remember that students should know what they need by this point in their school careers. Many students with disabilities will have received special education services, including accommodations, for years before coming to your class. They can speak about the experiences and what has helped them in the past and share information about how other teachers have provided accommodations. In fact, the ability to discuss and advocate for their needs is a good skill for college-bound students to have. See "Fostering Student Independence" below for prompts to help students identify accommodations that are helpful to them.

FOSTERING STUDENT INDEPENDENCE

Student, who knows what you need better than you do? Your advanced science class is the perfect opportunity for you to practice self-advocating for your classroom accommodations. Think about what helps you succeed in your courses. What changes have teachers made for you in the past that have helped you perform your best? Consider specifically the five categories listed below (Edgemon, Jablonski, and Lloyd 2006). We have listed just one question under each category, but accommodations should be based on what your IEP team, including you and your parents, decides you need, and should not be limited to this list.

- *Presentation accommodations:* Do you need someone to read instructions or content to you because of poor reading comprehension?
- *Time accommodations:* Do you need more time than your peers on tests to process the questions and formulate answers?
- *Setting accommodations:* Do you need to take assessments in a small group or with special lighting because of distractibility?
- *Response accommodations:* Do you need to express your knowledge in atypical ways, such as by dictating information or completing projects, due to writing difficulties?
- *Aid accommodations:* Do you need special assistive technology or low-tech aids like a calculator to keep pace with your peers, even though you can do the work?

Once your IEP team has decided, with your input, what accommodations are appropriate for you, take responsibility for having the accommodations you need. That may mean talking to your teachers, reminding them about your needs, or even setting up the procedures you will need to use to access the accommodation yourself.

Statement of Services

Finally, the IEP has several different parts that outline where the student will receive services. Students who are in your classes will likely be receiving very few intensive special education services. It is likely that they will be receiving consultative services, meaning that the special education teacher is providing support to the general education teachers but not working directly with the student, or that direct services are provided during basic skills or study hall. This part of the IEP is important for you to attend to so that you know where to go if the student needs support: Who should you talk to? What process is in place? Though your role is as general education teacher and your students should not require additional supports, you want to know what is available to them.

Learner Characteristics

Students with disabilities in your advanced science courses will most likely have mild disabilities. Most disability categories have a continuum, meaning that individuals with the same educational label may have a broad range of characteristics, but those students with disabilities who pursue advanced coursework are likely to fall into the mild end of the disability continuum (i.e., learning disabilities, emotional or behavioral disabilities, Asperger syndrome). In general, the students with disabilities who end up in your courses will be of average (or higher) intelligence, lack some social skills, lack ingrained study skills, and be motivated to succeed. In the following sections, we outline broad characteristics of nine of the disability categories outlined in special education law. See Figure 1.3 for examples of individuals in advanced science courses with some of these disabilities.

FIGURE 1.3. WHO WILL BE IN MY CLASS?

Here are some descriptions of a few students with disabilities you may find in your advanced-level science courses.

- Jack is a 15-year-old sophomore with a physical disability, cerebral palsy, which affects his motor movement. He can walk and write with a pencil, though not very legibly. He is as smart and cognitively capable as all of the other students in his honors-level physics class. Jack needs accommodations for note-taking, such as a laptop, and a patient and physically able lab partner to help with physical manipulation during lab work, as well as the ability to submit in-class assignments via e-mail from his laptop instead of as handwritten work.
- Bethany, a 16-year-old junior with a learning disability, is taking International Baccalaureate (IB) biology. She is very interested in the subject of this advanced-level class and highly motivated to do well. Her reading disability requires that she have extra time for in-class assignments that require reading, which her teacher typically accommodates by providing her with the reading the day before they will use it in class. Bethany also requires some organizational accommodations, including checklists for multistep tasks, such as when the class is doing dissection labs.
- Ralph is an 18-year-old senior in Advanced Placement (AP) chemistry. Ralph has Asperger's syndrome, which means that, among other characteristics, he takes things very literally and is easily thrown off his game, so to speak. His chemistry teacher provides a predictable schedule during both the class day (homework review, new instruction, group work, large-group review) and the class week (doing lab work on the same days of the week when possible). Ralph benefits from knowing about changes to this schedule in advance. Ralph also requires that large tasks be broken down and presented to him in smaller chunks, so during labs he has a special packet that shows only two or three steps at a time.

Specific Learning Disability

Specific learning disability (LD) is the largest disability category in schools today. The federal definition specifically states that students with SLD may have difficulty with the ability to listen, think, speak, read, write, spell, or do mathematical calculations (Hallahan, Kauffman, and Pullen 2012). Students who are in your advanced-level science courses will have mild impairments in these areas or will have learned strategies to work around the effect the disability has on their academic achievements. These strategies, such as specific note-taking methods, combined with IEP-mandated accommodations, will allow students with LD to be successful in your classroom.

Emotional Disturbance

Emotional disturbance (ED)—more often colloquially called emotional disorders or disabilities or behavioral disorders—is a very broad category that is difficult to define with clear lines regarding what it does and does not include. Some of the important definitional markers are an inability to build and maintain relationships, inappropriate behaviors and feelings, and pervasive unhappiness or depression (Hallahan, Kauffman, and Pullen 2012). We naturally think of people with overt, or acting-out, behaviors as having an ED. Oppositional defiant disorder, for example, is easier for most people to identify as an ED than, say, depression. You may have students with overt behaviors in your advanced class—typically, those who have built-in supports and have proven success in the general education classroom will be in your class—but you will probably have more students with covert behaviors such as depression, obsessive compulsive disorder, bipolar disorder, and anxiety.

Autism

As discussed above, all disabilities can be thought of as being on a continuum, but autism has the longest history of being thought of in this way, with Asperger's syndrome being on the mild end of the spectrum and the most likely medical label for students in your advanced science classes. The legal definition of autism references significant defects in verbal and nonverbal communication and social interaction. Students in your classes will be better at expressing themselves and understanding your communication, but also are likely to take directions and expressions literally ("I'll be with you in a minute" may be interpreted as 60 seconds and no longer); have difficulty interpreting emotion, facial expressions, and sarcasm; need advanced warning and time to acclimate to changes in schedule; and have difficulty interacting with peers (Hallahan, Kauffman, and Pullen 2012). Some students with Asperger's will fit right in with your class, barely standing out from their peers because they have learned good strategies; others will be quirky, not quite fitting in but perfectly capable and able to do the work, and you will appreciate them all!

Deafness and Hearing Impairment

Traditionally, we think of deafness as being a complete lack of ability to hear; however, the educational definition includes severe hearing loss, not only a complete absence of the ability to hear. Students may have some residual hearing, allowing them to hear muted noise though unable to understand and process spoken words, even with amplification (Hallahan, Kauffman, and Pullen 2012). In practical terms, this does mean that any students in your class who fall into this category will require extensive accommodation, for both safety (use of light when gaining student attention) and communication. Many students with severe hearing impairments may learn a form of sign language. If this is the case, it may behoove you to learn some of the most important signs to communicate directly with the student, but there likely will also be a sign language interpreter in the classroom to facilitate your communication. See Figure 1.4 for tips for working with an interpreter. If the student does not know sign language, or does not have an interpreter, you will want to create an environment where the student feels like he can ask you to repeat or slow down and where you use visuals whenever possible. Remember to face the student when speaking and to use whatever other accommodations are laid out in the IEP. It is also important to remember that accommodations require some interpretation. For instance, "preferential seating" may mean the location in the room varies, perhaps with the student sitting in the back of the room, away from the air conditioner, for lecture and near the front of the lab area, where there is less background noise.

FIGURE 1.4. TIPS FOR WORKING WITH AN INTERPRETER

- Direct your comments to the student, not the interpreter, when having an interpreted one-on-one conversation.
- Provide the interpreter with curriculum information ahead of time so he or she can prepare for the specific vocabulary and has a guide for lectures.
- Unless hired as such, an interpreter is not an aide and may not be a school system employee. If you do not know that the person is hired directly by the school as an instructional assistant, do not ask her to do things other than interpret, and do not leave her alone with the class.
- Be aware of lag time between your speaking and the student's understanding due to the interpretation time. If you ask the class a question and want to call on the student with the hearing impairment, give extra time.
- Be patient!

Source: University of Virginia. n.d.

Orthopedic Impairment

This educational category includes individuals with physical disabilities that affect movement. Examples include cerebral palsy, amputation, and fragile bone disorder, to name a few. The educational impact for these students hinges on their need for accommodation due to movement restrictions, which may be more prevalent in some classes than in others. For that matter, the effect may be greater on some days in your classroom than on others (Hallahan, Kauffman, and Pullen 2012).

Other Health Impairment

Other health impairment (OHI) is a broad category that can encompass everything from attention deficit hyperactivity disorder (ADHD) to AIDS to diabetes to kidney failure. Traditionally, this category was used for individuals with chronic health issues that required students to spend large amounts of time outside of school (Hallahan, Kauffman, and Pullen 2012). Though you may have a student like this in your classroom, it is unlikely that an IEP team will decide that it is reasonable for the rigor of your advanced classroom to adjust for a student who is not able to be in the classroom. It would be more likely that you may have a student who exhausts easily and so is only in school for part of the day. It is most likely that students with an OHI label in your classroom will have ADHD.

ADHD comes in three types: inattentive, hyperactive-impulsive, and combined (Hallahan, Kauffman, and Pullen 2012). What this means is that a student in your classroom with ADHD may present as overly energetic, having a hard time sitting still, but he also may present as a daydreamer who has difficulty staying on task, or a combination of the two characteristics. Typically, we focus on putting strategies in place to help the student stay focused and on task or providing opportunities for the student to move in appropriate ways throughout the class.

Traumatic Brain Injury

Teenagers are at high risk for developing traumatic brain injuries (TBI) due to not wearing a helmet, not using a seatbelt, or engaging in reckless behavior—basically, just being teenagers. TBI takes many forms, often resulting in cognitive impairment that would preclude a student from taking an advanced class, but sometimes having more physical, emotional, and social impacts. The biggest struggle for individuals who have a TBI is recognizing that they have an impairment at all (Hallahan, Kauffman, and Pullen 2012). You may find that a student with a TBI has come into your class thinking that he can sustain the workload, but then tires easily, has trouble with short-term memory, or cannot be objective about his lack of progress in class. If this happens, talk to the special educator to see if there are accommodations you can make in the classroom to help the student, or if your classroom is not an appropriate placement. TBI is a sudden change that is difficult for everyone involved to get a handle on, so it could be that the student can be successful with additional supports and it may just take some time to determine which supports are necessary.

Visual Impairment, Including Blindness

Many people have a preconceived notion that people with visual impairments, much like hearing impairments, completely lack one of their five senses. Again, though, this is not the case. A student with a visual impairment has a severe deficit in her vision but may have the ability to see things very close up with a lot of assistance. It is possible you may have individuals with visual impairments in your advanced class, and it will be important for you to review the IEP and work with the special educator to make sure your classroom is set up so the students can be successful.

Gifted and Talented

Though not a federally defined disability category, many states identify students with special talents or gifts (GT) and provide services to these students by writing an IEP. Other states identify the GT population and provide services based on state or local laws. You may be familiar with GT students and have experience teaching them. Students who the school has determined are GT with a disability that requires special education are often identified with the term *twice exceptional*, and they will have IEPs to address their disabilities (Hallahan, Kauffman, and Pullen 2012). Twice exceptional students are often difficult to identify, as their gifts or talents may mask their underlying disabilities (Hallahan, Kauffman, and Pullen 2012). These students may appear to be of average abilities because their disability affects their classroom functioning, thus hiding their special gifts or talents.

The characteristics of students who are twice exceptional are varied, and many share traits with GT students. However, here are some common concerns that have been mentioned with twice exceptional students: highly verbal though poor writing skills; strong observational skills, though often lacking in memory; poor reading ability; easily bored with some tasks; and difficulty paying attention unless highly motivated by the content (CEC 2011). Thus, it is important that you get to know the students and their individual abilities. Please ask the special education teacher if you have any questions or concerns about how the disability may be affecting the student's performance in your classroom. Please see Figure 1.5 (p. 14) for more information on resources for students who are both gifted and have a disability.

FIGURE 1.5. RESOURCES FOR TWICE EXCEPTIONAL STUDENTS

- The National Association for Gifted Children has many resources and materials for teachers of GT students. Their website is located at *www.nagc.org* and provides an excellent overview of how to incorporate best practices for this population of learners.
- The National Research Center on the Gifted and Talented at the University of Virginia provides research-based information on identifying and teaching GT students. Their website is located at *http://curry.virginia.edu/research/centers/nrcgt*.
- The Council for Exceptional Children (CEC) is the organization for students with disabilities, their parents, and educators. Their website (*www.cec.sped.org*) has many resources and materials for teachers of special needs children. It also provides resources for students who are twice exceptional. You can locate these resources by searching for the term *twice exceptional*. This website is well worth exploring when you have students with disabilities in your classroom.

It is a misperception that individuals with disabilities cannot be as smart as their nondisabled peers. In general, students with learning disabilities will have the same bell curve of intelligence as the general population (Hallahan, Kauffman, and Pullen 2012), and students who are not in the top half of that curve are unlikely to choose to take an advanced class (see Figure 1.6).

FIGURE 1.6. IQ AND THE BELL CURVE

IQ scores are reported as what is called a standard score with a normal distribution, meaning that the average score on an IQ test is 100 and the standard deviation is 15. Therefore, approximately 68% of the population will have an IQ ranging from 85 to 115 (or 100 ±15, or the standard deviation), and 95% of the population will have an IQ between 70 and 130 (or 100 ±30, or twice the standard deviation). (See Krathwohl 2009 for more information.)

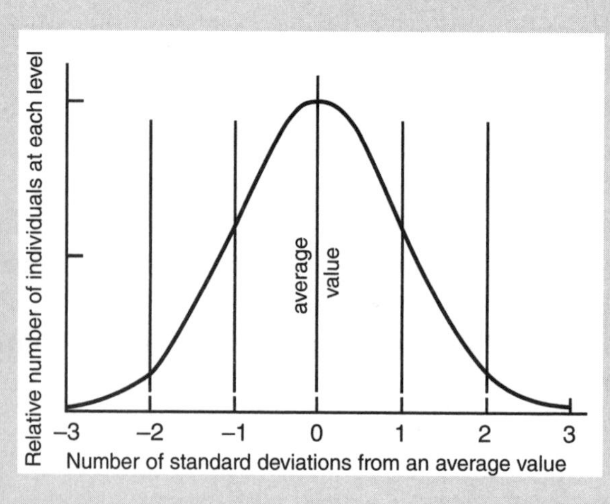

Students with disabilities can all, regardless of label, be deficient in social and study skills (Hallahan, Kauffman, and Pullen 2012). Social skills are problematic for a variety of reasons, but much of the issue comes down to the individual either not understanding the unwritten rules of social interaction or being unable to "read" other people (e.g., tone of voice, facial expressions). This inability can cause issues with communication between students and between yourself and the student with the disability. Study skills that students may struggle with include organization, note-taking skills, and time management. Reading the IEP will give you an idea of the student's proficiency in these areas, and throughout the book we provide ideas of how to work with students who struggle with social and study skills.

Once students with disabilities are assigned to your classroom, you need to find out more information about them. Please contact the special education teacher and review the IEP. The IEP will provide you with important information on the student's strengths and weaknesses, goals, and any needed accommodations, as discussed in this chapter. All of the information on the IEP is important and will provide you with information to begin your school year; however, you need to get to know the student (and how he or she performs) in your classroom to better adjust your instruction to meet his or her needs. Please see Figure 1.7 for some resources on science and students with disabilities.

FIGURE 1.7. RESOURCES ON SCIENCE AND STUDENTS WITH DISABILITIES

- Science Education for Students With Disabilities (*www.sesd.info/aboutus.htm*):
    - o Provides information on including students with specific disabilities
    - o Gives tips for making accommodations in your classroom
    - o Addresses concerns specific to the discipline (biology, Earth science, chemistry)
    - o Has a newsletter and a journal that you can review for helpful ideas
- The National Science Teachers Association (NSTA; *www.nsta.org*):
    - o Provides information on including students with disabilities in your classroom
    - o Includes resources that address curriculum issues and adaptations and accommodations needed by students with disabilities
    - o Has an online store with books and resources
- The College Board (*http://apcentral.collegeboard.com/apc/Controller.jpf*):
    - o Includes course-related materials, such as test preparation and sample test questions
    - o Provides resources by discipline (biology, chemistry, physics)
    - o Gives a discussion forum for teachers to share ideas and materials
    - o Lists links to other websites with helpful resources

Conclusion

Finally, it is important to remember that regardless of disability, students are more alike than not. Any student choosing to take an honors, AP, or IB course is going to have motivation to do well. Gallup reports that students in these classes are overwhelmingly motivated intrinsically and intend to go on to college, so they are taking advanced courses to better position themselves for admittance (*American Teacher* 2004). Though students with disabilities will need some special considerations, they are, at the core, just individual teenagers in your classroom, like the ones you have already been successful in reaching and teaching. Throughout the rest of this book, we will include specific considerations and suggestions for working with students with specific disabilities or deficits.

IDEAS TO GET YOU STARTED

Review your students' IEPs, specifically looking at the following parts:

- *PLOP:* Are there any tips you can use for working with the student? Make note of the student's interests and strengths to help make connections with the student. Be aware of the student's weaknesses and how your class may impact them.
- *Goals:* Will you need to be prepared to provide data to the special education case manager?
- *Case manager:* Take note of who the student's case manager is so you know who to go to with questions or concerns.
- *Accommodations:* Will you need help from the case manager to follow or interpret the accommodations?

References

American Teacher. 2004. Higher-level courses attracting students. *American Teacher* 88 (7): 2.

Bateman, B. D., and M. A. Linden. 2006. *Better IEPs: How to develop legally correct and educationally useful programs.* 4th ed. Verona, WI: Attainment.

Center for Applied Special Technology (CAST). 2010. *What is universal design for learning?* Wakefield, MA: CAST. *www.cast.org/reearch/udl/index.html*

Council for Exceptional Children (CEC). 2011. Twice exceptional. *www.cec.sped.org/AM/Template.cfm?Section=Twice_Exceptional&Template=/TaggedPage/TaggedPageDisplay.cfm&TPLID=37&ContentID=5634*

deBettencourt, L. U. 2002. Understanding the differences between IDEA and section 504. *Teaching Exceptional Children* 34 (3): 16–23.

Edgemon, E. A., B. J. Jablonski, and J. W. Lloyd. 2006. Large-scale assessments: A teacher's guide to making decisions about accommodations. *Teaching Exceptional Children* 38 (3): 6–11.

Fuchs, L. S., D. Fuchs, S. B. Eaton, C. Hamlett, E. Binkley, and R. Crouch. 2000. Using objective data sources to enhance judgments about test accommodations. *Exceptional Children* 67: 67–81.

Hallahan, D. P., J. M. Kauffman, and P. C. Pullen. 2012. *Exceptional learners: Introduction to special education.* 12th ed. Boston: Allyn & Bacon.

Kauffman, J. M., and D. P. Hallahan. 2005. *Special education: What it is and why we need it.* Boston: Allyn & Bacon.

Krathwohl, D. R. 2009. *Methods of educational and social science research: The logic of methods.* 3rd ed. Long Grove, IL: Waveland Press.

University of Virginia. n.d. *Faculty guide to accommodating students with disabilities.* Charlottesville, VA: University of Virginia.

CHAPTER 2

Working With the IEP Team

We provided background on individualized education programs (IEP) in Chapter 1, including why we have this legal document and what is included in the document. As with most legal documents, an IEP is only as good as its composition and follow-through. The fact that the IEP is legally binding holds the school accountable for the plan the IEP team has laid out, but if the plan is not solid, if there is not an opportunity for all of the important parties to have input, if the goals are not appropriate, and if the accommodations do not match the student's needs, then being accountable does not help the student. It is important that the IEP team keeps the focus of all discussion on what is best for the student—on what he or she needs to be able to be successful—and has good communication to occasionally check in and make sure the IEP is adequate and working.

Why are we telling you all of this? Because you are part of the IEP team and will bring valuable information about the demands of your classroom and the requirements involved in advanced science. Reflect on the IEP parts outlined in Chapter 1 and think about the kind of input you could bring to each piece, especially the accommodations. Later in this chapter, we discuss the transition plan, another piece of the IEP that will benefit from you sharing your knowledge and experience.

Who Is on the IEP Team?

An IEP team can be a very small, bare-bones group, or it can include enough people that no conference room is big enough for the meetings. At a minimum, the law requires that IEP teams include the student's parents, at least one general education teacher, at least one special education teacher, a school administrator, and the student when appropriate. The team may also include related service personnel, such as speech, physical, and occupational therapists; personnel involved with services the student is transitioning from or to (e.g., early childhood services or postsecondary education agencies); and anyone else that the parents and the school deem should be present, including parent advocates (Bateman and Linden 2006).

Parents

Arguably the most important people at the table in an IEP meeting, if the student is not present, are the parents. Often only one parent will attend, and if there are no parents, at least one legal guardian must attend. The presence of a parent or legal guardian is important because he or she must sign off on the educational program; we cannot begin or change services without their approval (Bateman and Linden 2006). Though you may hear horror stories in the hallway about parents being unhappy with the school and IEP meetings being contentious, parents are usually satisfied with communication and dealings in IEP meetings, though less satisfied in secondary schools than in elementary schools, with curriculum programming being the most common point of contention (Fish 2008). This means that the most common disagreement is about where and what the student should be learning—for instance, whether the student should be in your advanced science class or in a general education class. Parents often push to have their child in classes that may not be appropriate for them given background knowledge, academic achievement history, and disability.

General Education Teacher

If you were wondering where you came in, wonder no longer! The law requires that at least one general education teacher be part of the IEP team. The intention is that there needs to be someone present who is highly knowledgeable about the curriculum involved in the discussions to ensure the student can access the curriculum. Legally, this should be a general educator who works with the student, though not all of the general educators who work with the student need to be invited or attend the meeting. Case law encourages schools to invite input from all of the general educators who work with the student, even if they are not able to attend the meeting (Bateman and Linden 2006).

This requirement for teachers who have knowledge of the student typically means that one of the student's current teachers attends the IEP meeting, and the special educator seeks information from the student's other teachers in drafting the PLOP and goals for the coming year (see Chapter 1 for more information about the IEP parts). However, it is important to involve individuals who know the curriculum the student will be learning, not just those who know the student, so it would be appropriate for you to attend an IEP meeting for a student you do not yet know but who aspires to take your advanced science class.

You might come to an IEP meeting to discuss the advanced nature of your science class, including doing labs and the importance of homework completion. You can provide examples of worksheets, tests, and materials to help promote the discussion of whether placement in your class would be appropriate for this student and to set expectations. For a student who has been in your class all year, you can provide input into the transition plan (discussed later in this chapter), such as skills the student should continue to work on to be successful in college courses.

Special Education Teacher

Though the culture varies from district to district and school to school, most of the time the special educator who is part of the IEP team will be the student's "case manager." This means that the special education teacher will be coordinating communication, gathering data, and spearheading the IEP writing process. This will also be the person you and the student should go to if you have questions about what services or accommodations the student should be receiving, concerns about the student's progress, or ideas about how to help the student succeed. The special educator is responsible for implementing the IEP (Bateman and Linden 2006). In some cases, the special education teacher can provide individual support for a student through a basic skills or resource class. This might include help with organization of assignments, preparation for class, and the use of assistive technologies. Once a student with a disability is assigned to your class, make sure to check in with the special education teacher.

School Administrator

The school administrator, or a designee, serves the role of school district representative at IEP meetings. This person must have the authority to commit school district resources that the IEP team defines, and not be overridden by someone above them (Bateman and Linden 2006). For students you will work with, there should be no issue about the school's fiscal ability to provide appropriate services. The only time that there may be intense discussion about the fiscal impact of a student's needs for your classroom would be if the student needed intense assistive technology. Please note that if the IEP team decides a student needs a particular accommodation, cost cannot be a reason that the school does not provide it. However, the school and the IEP team can consider alternatives that meet the same accommodation need at a lower cost. For instance, a student who needs to type instead of hand write could use a laptop computer as an accommodation, but he could use an AlphaSmart device with many of the same capabilities at a fraction of the price.

Student

The law provides a lot of flexibility about whether or not the student needs to be at the IEP meeting, until a certain age. Federal law requires students to attend starting at 16 years old (earlier in some states), but they are encouraged to attend earlier with parental permission (Bateman and Linden 2006). Given this, it is highly likely that students will be in any IEP meeting you will attend. The student's presence is important, especially if the student is ready to be involved in the meeting, because she can provide feedback and information on strengths, weaknesses, and what she wants. Additionally, student involvement will likely lead to more student compliance (i.e., using accommodations) and better self-advocacy skills (see "Student Self-Advocacy" [p. 27] and McGahee, Mason, Wallace, and Jones 2001).

Optional Invitees

The phrase "It takes a village to raise a child" is sometimes very true for providing a proper education for students with disabilities. Depending on what the student's disability and its severity, it is possible that many related service personnel will be present at IEP meetings. This can include speech therapists (for students who have language and communication disorders), occupational therapists (for students with fine motor issues), and physical therapists (for students with large motor issues). You may also have an adapted PE teacher, itinerant teachers who specialize in the student's disability (especially if the student has a low-incidence disability such as vision or hearing impairment), or behavior specialists. These individuals bring their specialty background knowledge to the IEP team to help meet all of the educational needs of the student (Bateman and Linden 2006).

But our IEP conference table is not too full yet! The above parties can be part of the IEP team at the school's request because they have substantial knowledge of the child, as can a language interpreter if the parent and school require one. Additionally, parents can invite anyone they want to be there who has substantial knowledge of the child (Bateman and Linden 2006). This may mean additional family, often a benefit if the parent has limited understanding of school structure, or it may mean professionals such as parent advocates, lawyers, and independent doctors. Remember, just because a parent does not choose to come to the meeting alone does not automatically mean the IEP meeting will be painful and prolonged—if you did not have context for what was happening at the meeting and you were the only non-school personnel there, wouldn't you want some backup?

Transition Plans

The IEP parts listed in Chapter 1 are required for all IEPs, but once students turn 16, the IEP team is required to include a transition plan, though they may choose to include this earlier and state law may require including it prior to age 16. The goal of the transition plan is to think ahead to what the student will do after high school and set goals related to postsecondary training, education, employment, and, if appropriate, independent living. The transition plan will also lay out goals for the student while he is in high school to work toward the postsecondary goals and include a statement related to the student's knowledge of his rights upon reaching the age of majority, the age at which he legally becomes an adult (Bateman and Linden 2006). When students reach the age of majority, the legal rights that his parents have held with regard to the student's education and IEP are transferred to the student; though we continue to include parents and want to have their input and support, the student's signature is the one that is all-powerful once he reaches age 18 (Bateman and Linden 2006).

As an IEP team thinks about postsecondary goals for a student, it is important to think about academic and work life, but also social life and home life, which tend to be overlooked when planning for students with learning disabilities, leading students to be less satisfied with their transition in these areas (Daviso, Denney, Baer, and Flexer 2011). You may assume that students in your advanced science classes are college bound, which is probably true, and that they will not need transition services as they prepare for postsecondary life, which is not true. Even those who are college bound may need instruction in nonacademic areas to succeed in college. Additionally, many students make the choice to attend school and work part-time to lessen the financial burden of a postsecondary education or give them more time to discover what they want to be when they grow up. See Table 2.1 for examples of long-term goals and the matching transition services an IEP team may include in a transition plan.

TABLE 2.1. POSTSCHOOL GOALS AND TRANSITION SERVICES

Sample Postschool Goal	Sample Transition Services
Work full- or part-time (employment)	• Assist student in obtaining work while in high school. • Engage student in a service-learning project (O'Connor 2009). • Expose student to a variety of potential future careers.
Attend a two-year college (education)	• Research local options and admission requirements and processes. • Research process for obtaining accommodations. • Pursue coursework for an academic diploma.
Attend a four-year college (education)	• Same as those for a two-year college, plus: • Prepare for and take the SAT or ACT. • Attend college fairs and visit colleges.
Engage in social activities (community participation)	• Join extracurricular activities such as a sport (as a manager, if lacking athletic ability) or club.
Use public transportation (community participation)	• Review bus and/or subway routes. • Take field trips that include using public transportation.
Make good fiscal decisions related to debt (e.g., credit cards, ATMs)	• Enroll in personal finance class.

Transition plans vary greatly depending on the student's disability and needs because they, like the entire IEP, are individualized. However, in general, transition plans for students who are in your classes will be shorter and less involved than for students who have more severe disabilities. Your knowledge and experience are important in crafting the plan for future academics. You have deep knowledge of the academic demands in your field and of colleges that have strong programs in your area of specialty. Because the nature of AP and IB courses is that they are college-level, you also have a greater ability to speak to your current students' needs before they go to college: Do they need to improve study skills? Do they need to work on self-advocacy?

Besides being a part of developing the plan, it is important for you to know the transition plans for students who come into your classroom so that you can enhance and provide additional opportunities to practice the needed transition skills. If you know you have students in your class who want to study your field in college, working in conversations about good matches would be appropriate. Or if you know the student needs to work on work skills such as accepting direction from peers, you can talk to the special educator about how to provide support for this goal in your classroom.

Communication With the IEP Team

As noted above, all general education teachers are not necessarily required or even invited to attend IEP meetings for students in their classes. Given the importance of your knowledge of curriculum content and the fact that you will be legally required to follow the IEP whether or not you are in the meeting, we strongly recommend you make every attempt to be a part of the IEP team. The special educators in your school may not be used to general educators being excited about being on an IEP team, so you will need to clearly communicate your desire to them. We suggest talking to the special education department chair, or sending e-mails to all special educators who may be case managers for students eligible to come into your class (e.g., juniors for a senior-level class), and requesting that you be invited to IEP meetings if they have reason to believe the student will be in your advanced class the following year. You are not being confrontational or a thorn in someone's side; in fact, the special educator should be happy to have you offer your availability! They know that with you involved early on, the student is more likely to be successful in your advanced-level course.

The actual scheduling of IEP meetings happens differently from school to school. There are some schools that have someone centrally who will schedule the meeting, with little consultation with you. This meeting might take place before or after school or during your planning period, or perhaps a substitute or another teacher can fill in for you while you are at the meeting. In other schools, the case manager will schedule the meeting and work with all parties to come up with a time that works for everyone. Please be flexible with your schedule, recognizing that coordinating so many schedules is a difficult task and sometimes meetings cannot be scheduled at an ideal time for you. If you absolutely are not able to attend an IEP meeting, please do provide some information, in writing, that can be shared at the meeting. See Figure 2.1 for a list of information to include to help the IEP team understand the demands of your class.

FIGURE 2.1. THINGS TO SHARE WITH THE IEP TEAM

- Your course syllabus
- Explanation of the physical tasks required (e.g., working with knives, fire, chemicals)
- List of potential field trips and associated goals
- Your expectations regarding homework and classwork (amounts per night and per week; if there are activities you typically have students do in class that are timed)
- Behavioral expectations for working with peers
- Format of the end-of-course assessment (AP or IB) and what (if anything) you know about accommodations for that assessment

When you attend an IEP meeting, it is likely that the team will be in a conference room sitting around a big table. You may know most of the people at the table, and most meetings will begin with introductions, but it is good for you to go ahead and introduce yourself to those you do not know, including parents and the student. As the meeting begins and progresses, please do not hesitate to share pertinent information—this may be information the IEP team needs as they decide what the student needs to be successful in your advanced science class (see Figure 2.1) or, if you have already had the student in class, it may be information related to how the student is functioning and specific information about supports the student needs. Please feel free to share samples of student projects, homework, and other materials that provide a "snapshot" of the student's progress in your class. As the IEP team discusses goals and accommodations, if you do not understand something, please ask. Special educators often talk in "special education-ease," and it is likely that if you do not know a term, the parent also does not know it. You will be responsible for following accommodations from the IEP, so if they are not clear to you, be sure to seek clarification.

As stated in Chapter 1, it is likely that students in your advanced classes will not have academic goals that are relevant to their time with you. Instead, they may have social, behavioral, or study skills goals to work on while they are in your classroom. You may have a hand in crafting these goals or deciding which behaviors are priorities. It is most likely, however, that your role in IEP goals will be to provide occasional information about the goal behavior. The law requires that the school regularly and consistently provide parents updates on student progress toward IEP goals (U.S. Department of Education 2004). This progress reporting is usually part of the special education teacher's responsibilities, but you are the one with knowledge about how the student is doing in your class, so plan to keep the special educator "in the loop." You may initiate these conversations ("Mrs. Smith, I'm concerned about James's calling out behavior"), or the special educator may request specific information. It is best when the IEP team decides how the goal will be monitored and data will be collected when they write the goal. See Table 2.2 for examples of goal behaviors and data collection.

TABLE 2.2. GOAL AND DATA COLLECTION EXAMPLES

Goal Behavior	Data Collection
Turning in homework	Your grade book
On-task behavior	Special education teacher observations
Calling out, raising hand, making inappropriate comments	Choose a data collection day and keep a tally of the behavior on that day. You can keep the tally by making marks on paper, moving paper clips from one pocket to another, or using any other method that is least intrusive to your teaching style.
Appropriate peer interactions	Have all students fill out reflection pages after group work, reflecting on their own contributions and behavior and those of their peers. Jot down your own observations on the student's page when it is complete.

Communication With the Parent

Ongoing communication with parents of students with disabilities will help alleviate potential conflicts, and you should provide regular updates to the special education teacher to pass on to the parents or to the parents directly through a note home or via e-mail. While this is not typically needed in the advanced, accelerated, or honors classroom, parents of students with disabilities are used to frequent communication about their child from teachers. You absolutely may contact parents directly, especially if you have concerns or praise. Remember that parents of students with disabilities most often get calls when things go wrong or their child is struggling. Try to make your first contact with parents positive, as early positive interactions with parents will make it easier to collaborate if the student struggles later in the school year.

Student Self-Advocacy

As discussed in the text introduction, self-advocacy is a key skill for personal success. Self-advocacy is part of the larger concept of self-determination, which is "being the causal agent in decisions and choices that have an impact on one's life" (Wehmeyer, Agran, and Hughes 1998, p. 6). Test et al. (2005) have determined that self-advocacy is composed of knowledge of self, knowledge of rights, communication skills, and leadership skills; leadership skills are most closely associated with student involvement in IEP meetings and transition planning. These are the areas in which we need to help students during the high school years so that they are ready to be self-advocates when they leave high school, if not while in high school. One of the most appropriate ways for students to work on self-advocacy skills is to be involved in running their IEP meeting. The special educator works with the student on the skills required to lead the meeting, but it is important to have support from all of the teachers. See "Fostering Student Independence" (p. 28) for ideas to share with students to prompt them to think about these four areas of self-advocacy.

When you view the components of self-advocacy skills, it should be clear that these are skills every student—with or without disabilities—must have to be successful in college. We have evidence that self-advocacy skills are important to success behaviorally (Sebag 2010), in work, and in postsecondary education (Madaus, Faggella-Luby, and Dukes 2011). Behaviorally, students will have greater buy-in to an intervention if they have a part in setting their goals and responsibility for tracking their progress (Sebag 2010). Though students with disabilities may have the ability to receive some of the same accommodations in college that they received in high school, the onus is entirely on them to contact the college's disability office, provide appropriate documentation, and then talk with professors about how to go about using the accommodations in class. This change in ownership from case manager to student is only successful if the student has self-advocacy skills and can take on an active and responsible role in obtaining the services they need (Hadley 2011). You have the opportunity to help students hone their self-advocacy skills while they are in your classroom so they can have greater success when they move on to college.

FOSTERING STUDENT INDEPENDENCE

Student, it is important for you to have the skills to speak up for yourself as you are in the general education classroom, and especially as you get ready to leave high school, because you will not have a case manager to speak up on your behalf when you go into the workplace or on to college. Think about the following questions, broken up into four dimensions of a skill called self-advocacy, and reflect on your ability to advocate for your needs.

Self-Advocacy Dimension	In Relation to Accommodations ...	Other Questions to Ask Yourself
Knowledge of self	• What are my strengths and weaknesses? • What helps me do better in class? • What helps me do better on tests and quizzes? • What accommodations am I resistant to using? Why?	• What are my interests? • What do I like to do? • What are my goals (in school, in life)?
Knowledge of rights	• Do I know what to do and who to talk to if my teacher does not let me use an accommodation on my IEP?	• Do I know when I can speak for myself, instead of someone else speaking for me? • Do I know my general rights as a member of the community?
Communication skills	• Am I comfortable telling my teachers what I need in the classroom? • Can I create, or have my case manager help me create, a template for this discussion? • Do I know who to talk to if I think I need a change in accommodations?	• Can I talk to my teachers to gather information about my strengths and weaknesses? • Do I listen when people talk about my faults?
Leadership skills	• Am I ready to talk about my needs related to accommodations at my IEP meeting? • Can I set up a process for using my accommodations (e.g., reserving a room in the counselor's office for testing)?	• Do I know the roles of my IEP team members? • Is there information I want to share at my IEP meeting or pieces of the IEP I want to present or handle?

Source: Test et al. 2005

Recognizing the importance of self-advocacy skills is just one part of the equation for success. We also have to be ready and knowledgeable about ways to teach or encourage students to be self-advocates. Consider the ideas in Figure 2.2. The IEP team should be thinking about ways to enhance a student's self-advocacy skills while writing the transition plan, but you should consider opportunities for students to be self-advocates in your classroom every day.

FIGURE 2.2. HOW YOU CAN ENCOURAGE SELF-ADVOCACY

- Encourage students to think about how their behaviors (study skills) played a role in their success (or lack thereof) on assessments.
- Encourage students to challenge the fairness of policies in your classroom. You may learn that you have been calling on the people in the front of the room more, and students will learn how to verbalize their concerns in a cogent way.
- As the IEP team deems appropriate, encourage students to be in charge of their own accommodations.
- Wait for students to ask for help before stepping in, when possible.
- Refer students to appropriate resources or encourage them to turn to resources sometimes instead of answering all questions immediately.
- When praising students for specific academic behaviors, make links to life applications. For instance, you can say, "Johnny, you have such a good grasp of this cellular respiration unit. I bet you would make a great cancer researcher!"

Conclusion

It is important to remember that you are a vital member of the IEP team, you bring unique knowledge and perspective, and communication with the rest of the team will lead to the best possible outcome for students with disabilities in your advanced science class. Communicating with so many people outside of your classroom may not be your modus operandi, but you will find that collaborating with the IEP team will lead to a more fulfilling experience for you and your students with disabilities.

IDEAS TO GET YOU STARTED

- Plan to attend an IEP meeting.
- Find out who the case manager is for your students with disabilities, and make a plan to get together with them.
- Brainstorm ways to link the work in your classroom to future job opportunities.

References

Bateman, B. D., and M. A. Linden. 2006. *Better IEPs: How to develop legally correct and educationally useful programs.* Verona, WI: Attainment.

Daviso, A. W., S. C. Denney, R. M. Baer, and R. Flexer. 2011. Postschool goals and transition services for students with learning disabilities. *American Secondary Education* 39: 77–93.

Fish, W. W. 2008. The IEP meeting: Perceptions of parents of students who receive special education services. *Preventing School Failure* 53 (1): 8–14.

Hadley, W. M. 2011. College students with disabilities: A student development perspective. *New Directions for Higher Education* 154: 77–81.

Madaus, J. W., M. N. Faggella-Luby, and L. Dukes, III. 2011. The role of non-academic factors in the academic success of college students with learning disabilities. *Learning Disabilities* 17: 77-82.

McGahee, M., C. Mason, T. Wallace, and B. Jones. 2001. *Student-led IEPs: A guide for student involvement*. Arlington, VA: Council for Exceptional Children.

O'Connor, M. P. 2009. Service works! Promoting transition success for students with disabilities through participation in service learning. *Teaching Exceptional Children* 41 (6): 13–17.

Sebag, R. 2010. Behavior management through self-advocacy: A strategy for secondary students with learning disabilities. *Teaching Exceptional Children* 42 (6): 22–29.

Test, D. W., C. H. Fowler, W. M. Wood, D. M. Brewer, D. M., and S. Eddy. 2005. A conceptual framework for self-advocacy for students with disabilities. *Remedial & Special Education* 26 (1): 43–54.

Wehmeyer, M. L., M. Agran, and C. Hughes. 1998. *Teaching self-determination to students with disabilities.* Baltimore, MD: Brookes.

CHAPTER 3

Classroom Considerations: Behavior

Though many teachers indicate that behavior management is a major challenge in their classroom, as an advanced science teacher you probably have fewer behaviors to deal with than some of your colleagues do. However, the idea of having students like we describe in Chapter 1 in your class may make you nervous if you think the behaviors will suddenly become an issue in your classroom. First, let us assure you that the IEP team would not place a student in your class if they did not fully believe the student could succeed in your classroom. Second, this chapter will provide you with tools and important vocabulary to understand how best to approach a student who does have behavioral challenges—the best way to deal with behaviors is to be consistent across settings, so work with the special educator to find out what has worked in other classrooms.

Though it is possible you will have behavioral concerns or considerations for any student in your classroom, those with learning disabilities and tactile disabilities (hearing and vision impairments) will generally be less likely to exhibit problem behavior than those with other disabilities; in terms of behavior, they will often look just like your students without disabilities. Students on the autism spectrum and those with emotional disabilities or ADHD, as we discussed in Chapter 1, may require some behavioral supports so they can be academically successful in your classroom. Do not assume that all of your students with disabilities will have behavior problems. Do not assume that all of your students with autism and emotional disabilities will have behavior problems; in fact, it is likely that most will not. Do be aware of how your behaviors and interactions affect the behavior of your students. There are often many things we cannot control in our classroom, but we can control our own behavior, which has a huge effect on the rest of the class. See Figure 3.1 (p. 32) for examples of behavioral choices teachers make.

Before you read the strategies and tips in the rest of the chapter, take a few minutes to think about the potential problem areas and times in your classroom. See Figure 3.2 (p. 33) for some ideas. Reflect on your years of experience: Have you

FIGURE 3.1. MAKING GOOD TEACHER BEHAVIOR CHOICES

Students respond to a teacher's behavior, and sometimes students behave to elicit a particular teacher reaction. It is important that you remember your actions and reactions can change the flow of your classroom and your behavior is the only behavior you can truly control.

Student Behavior	Appropriate Teacher Response	Less Effective Teacher Response
The student makes a joke at the teacher's expense.	Ignore, laugh along, redirect. In short, do what you tell your students to do if they are bullied.	Punish. Turn it around and make the student the butt of the joke.
The student argues that something you marked wrong on a paper (and is wrong) is correct.	Show the correct answer, offer to demonstrate how you got that answer, then move on. If the student is combative, it is likely he will not hear anything you say until he calms down.	Continue to engage the student, arguing that you are right.
The student is playing with something inappropriate in his desk.	Surreptitiously approach the student, take the object, and let the student know he can have it back later. When it is convenient, talk to the student about the behavior.	Stop your instruction and yell at the student in front of the rest of the class.

had students who have had a hard time following directions or who have gotten into conflict with you or their classmates? What were the circumstances? When have you noticed students get frustrated with tasks? Knowing when students may have difficulty leads to better preparation to avoid behavior problems.

Behavior Contracts

A contract, as you know, is a binding agreement between two or more persons or parties. You may use a type of contract with all of your students at the beginning of the year, laying out expectations and consequences for criteria such as lab behavior or homework. Please see Chapter 7 for an example of a Learning Contract that can be used for *all* of your students. The idea behind a behavior contract for students with disabilities is that the teacher and the student—sometimes with input from and in agreement with other members of the IEP team, such as a special educator or parents—create an agreement, often with a tit-for-tat reward. Depending on

FIGURE 3.2. POTENTIAL PROBLEMS IN THE CLASSROOM

- *Transitions:* This includes the transition into the classroom (What are students supposed to do when they come into class?), movements within the classroom (If all students move to the lab area at the same time, is it safe?), and switching from one task to another (What do students put away? What do they get out?).
- *Group work:* Group work might cause problems because of the student's interpersonal skills or because you are not able to oversee the entire room at the same time.
- *Timing of tasks:* Do you have a plan for if some students finish a task very early or very late in the class period?
- *Lack of structure:* Do students know what is expected of them? Do you have routines set up so expectations are clear?
- *Classroom organization:* Are the materials for labs easily accessible, or are there "bottle necks" as students start labs? Are there enough materials for every student or group? Is there enough personal space between students so that they can easily use notebooks or materials? Do students have a place to put their personal items? Can they find the safety equipment (goggles) easily?

whether or not the student meets certain behavioral expectations, he receives a reward or consequence as laid out in the contract. He can receive a reward for an increase in appropriate behavior or decrease in inappropriate behavior, for instance, or a consequence if he does not meet the expectations. When working with most students with disabilities, however, it is a good rule of thumb to only work in positives such as rewards.

The contract itself will have three major components: target behavior, a tracking process, and consequences (Cook 2005). For a contract to be effective, the behavior has to be meaningfully defined in a way that will enable all parties to recognize it. For instance, if "talking out" is the behavior, teachers who have a very tight definition of the term may include choral responses as talking-out behavior. Someone with a looser conception of the behavior, however, may only count a vocalization as talking out if there was no question posed to which the student could respond. It is also best for the behavior to be stated as a positive, such that the student's challenge is to increase appropriate behavior, instead of focusing on the negative behavior. For example, you could say, "Raise your hand" rather than "Stop calling out."

Tracking is important so that you and the student know if the student is meeting the terms in the contract. Think of this as data collection, and in fact a good tracking system can be supplied to the special educator as evidence of the student's progress towards a goal (see Chapter 2). The biggest challenge with a tracking system is to find something that will not make the student stand out from classmates. The special educator can help you develop appropriate systems, but suggestions include student self-monitoring with a discrete checklist at his or her seat, the teacher making discrete tallies on a piece of paper, and the teacher keeping a tally counter handy and clicking it when the behavior occurs. See Figure 3.3 for two sample behavior contracts—one geared toward specific student actions and one geared toward a more academic behavior of completing homework.

FIGURE 3.3. BEHAVIORAL CONTRACT

I, ______, am working on raising my hand and waiting to be called on in class. Even when I am very excited, I need to control my behavior by not calling out, but raising my hand instead. The teacher will tally the number of times that I raise my hand and the number of times I fail to raise my hand at least once a week. If I raise my hand more times than I call out, I can help the P.E. teacher with equipment during study hall on Friday each week in the first grading period.

____________________	________	____________________	________
Student Signature	Date	Teacher Signature	Date

Homework Contract

I, _____, recognize the importance of doing homework as practice for the material covered in class. The teacher, _____, agrees to allow me to complete abbreviated homework assignments, determined at her discretion and to include no fewer than one problem of each type. I agree to complete the assigned homework on time, following all appropriate directions, and without complaint. If I turn in 95% of the homework assignments on time, accurately, and having followed all directions for the first semester, the teacher and I will renegotiate the amount and type of homework I am required to do.

____________________	________	____________________	________
Student Signature	Date	Teacher Signature	Date

Positive Behavior Support

If your school uses positive behavior support (PBS), sometimes called positive behavior interventions and support (PBIS), then you likely know what this method is and are familiar with your school-level behavioral expectations and consequences, giving you a starting place for working with students with behavioral issues in your classroom. Even if your school, grade, or department does not use PBS, understanding the principles can help you when you work with students with behavioral difficulties and you can choose to use PBS in your classroom.

The basic premise behind PBS is that we should prevent inappropriate behavior instead of reacting to it. In your classroom, the most important thing you can do is create a comfortable, safe environment where students feel safe emotionally (Hendley 2007). To do this, be an active listener, remember that even high schoolers appreciate praise for appropriate behavior (e.g., "You all are doing a great job working in groups today!"), and encourage students to ask questions (Solar 2011). It is also important to create a structured environment in the classroom and to be consistent; students cannot meet expectations if they don't know the expectations. See Figure 3.4 for specific examples of ways to create a positive environment in your classroom so you can be more proactive than reactive.

FIGURE 3.4. BE PROACTIVE WITH BEHAVIOR

- Have clear rules posted, with expectations phrased positively. For example, use respectful language instead of inappropriate words.
- Compliment your students on appropriate behavior, being specific about the behavior. If you say "Johnny's doing a great job," you miss an opportunity to reinforce what the rest of the students should be doing.
- Be aware of students with covert (quiet, nondisruptive) behaviors and refer to their IEP for ideas on how best to engage them in class.
- Give students clear, complete directions, such as "Open your book to page 24 and read pages 24 and 25 silently, getting out pencil and paper when you are done."
- Avoid idle time. Students need to know what they should do if they finish a task before their peers.
- Have well-planned instruction. Good instruction is the first defense against misbehavior.
- Invest time in getting to know your students. Teachers who value relationships with their students have less uncooperative behavior in their classroom (Gregory and Ripski 2008).

Behavior Plans

Though not commonplace for students included in the general education classroom, the IEP team must create a behavior plan for any student whose behavior "impedes his or her own learning or that of others" (Bateman and Linden 2006, p. 80). This plan can take several different forms and is sometimes called a behavior intervention plan. For some students, definitely those whose behavior leads to suspension for ten days over the course of the year but also other students whose behavior may be hard to nail down, the IEP team will complete a functional behavior assessment (FBA) before writing the behavior plan. The purpose of FBA is to determine the function of student behavior so teachers can develop strategies to change the behavior. Typically, this is done through observation of the defined behavior and ends with manipulating antecedents or consequences to replace or decrease the behavior (Scott, Alter, and McQuillan 2010).

What this means for you is that a student may come into your classroom with a behavior plan in place, based on an FBA, so designed to alter a known behavior. For instance, last year, the IEP team conducted an FBA and determined that Frank's inappropriate behavior (engaging peers in discussion) typically occurred when Frank didn't know what he was supposed to be doing or was not sure how to proceed with the task (the antecedents). The IEP team created a behavior plan that included teaching Frank strategies for asking for help or indicating that he needed help in appropriate ways. You will want to read the behavior plan to know what strategies Frank should be using so you can prompt him if he forgets, as well as to understand the positive and negative consequences that are in place through the behavior plan.

Working With the IEP Team

In most cases, students will come into your classroom with strategies and plans already laid out. The IEP team will have spent time working on ideas, and the special education team will have taught the student how to use appropriate strategies to control their behavior. You will want to learn what these strategies are so you can remind students to use their strategies and prompt them with the steps if they are struggling. See Figure 3.5 for an example of a strategy students may have been taught for controlling their behavior and "Fostering Student Independence" for prompts to help students self-monitor.

FIGURE 3.5. STRATEGY EXAMPLE

One strategy for problem solving that students may have been taught to use is the acronym DIRT.

- **D**: Define the problem
- **I**: Identify choices
- **R**: Reflect on the choices
- **T**: Try it out!

Source: Cook 2005.

However, there may also be times when a student begins to exhibit behaviors in your classroom that did not exist in other settings, were not problematic in other

FOSTERING STUDENT INDEPENDENCE: SELF-MONITORING

Don't you hate it when the teacher has to call you out for your behavior? You spoke out of turn, weren't paying attention, or were playing with something in your desk, but having the teacher point out your behavior can be embarrassing. You can use something called self-monitoring to help decrease the number of times you aren't doing what you're supposed to be doing. Follow these steps, with help from your teachers. Research shows us that this works with high school students like you! (Graham-Day, Gardner, and Hsin 2010)

- Decide on the behavior to monitor. This should be a behavior that impedes your learning or the learning of others in the classroom. Define the behavior such that you will be consistent ("I only popped out of my chair to pick up an eraser from the floor; does that count as being out of my seat?"). When possible, phrase the behavior as a positive—you will feel much better about yourself if you are counting the things you are doing right rather than those you need to improve. Your teachers can help you define what is appropriate.
- Think about how to track or monitor your behavior.
  - How often will you check the behavior? Some behaviors (raising hand) can be counted every time they occur, while it is best to use a sampling method for other behaviors. For instance, were you on task for the entire last five minutes of class?
  - How will you record the behavior? Keeping a tally will be appropriate for most behaviors, but you will need a reminder of the time period if you are taking data every few many minutes. One idea is to download an app to your phone that will set off a timer (on vibrate only!) in prescribed intervals. Be sure to get permission if you are going to use any technology that may otherwise be considered contraband.
  - You want to be consistent and accurate in tracking your behavior. Talk to your classroom teacher to see if he or she, or maybe a friend, can track the behavior for a few days so you can compare results.
- Reflect on how self-monitoring is changing your behavior.
  - Graph the data from your tracking system. That should help you visualize the inappropriate behaviors decreasing and the appropriate behaviors increasing.
  - Consider other things that may be affected by your behavior change. For instance, did your grades go up? Is it easier to do group work?
  - If you don't see a lot of change, think about setting a specific goal with a reward for yourself. Maybe spending half an hour less studying one night and instead playing a video game.

Source: Rafferty 2010.

settings, or do not respond to the same interventions as in the past. Any time a student with an identified disability is struggling in your classroom, you need to communicate with the special education teacher. If behaviors are disruptive, the IEP team may meet to discuss altering the BIP. It is probable that someone will come into your class to observe and take data or that the special educator or school psychologist will provide you with questionnaires and forms to help define the behavior and determine the function of the behavior. The IEP team can help you brainstorm strategies to put in place to change or extinguish the behavior.

Medication

If the student is on medication, it is even more important that you communicate with the IEP team and parents about changes you see in behaviors. Please note that the school (including teachers and members of the IEP team) should *never* recommend or endorse that a student take medication. Decisions about medications need to be made by a medical doctor, and no one in the school is qualified to make recommendations about medical functions. However, when parents make teachers aware of changes in medications, then it is very helpful for teachers to communicate changes in behavior so that parents can work with the medical doctor to make appropriate medication decisions. Again, this is so important that we have to repeat it: Do not recommend that students take medications.

As you are probably aware from personal experience, medications often have side effects, ranging from those that have very little impact on daily life (e.g., hair loss) to those that can affect a person's behavior just as much as the medication can (e.g., fatigue, hunger, thirst). Though adolescents are often very sleepy because of their sleeping habits, do be aware that this is a common side effect of medications used for various emotional disabilities, ADHD, and autism. If you know that the student is on medication, you may need to cut him or her a little slack because yawning and drowsiness may not be the student's fault. The student also may really be extra thirsty or hungry and need the extra trip to the water fountain or bag of chips before class starts, though you may naturally be concerned that they are avoiding class activities.

Just because a particular behavior may be linked to medication doesn't mean that you have to ignore it no matter the effect on the class. Instead, you can accommodate the behavior. As you think about changes you can make in your classroom, remember to be a creative problem-solver. Although you may not normally allow food or drinks, maybe you can institute a "first five minutes" rule that allows all students to eat or drink for the first five minutes of class (as long as they clean up after themselves, don't go into lab areas, and follow other guidelines). Maybe a student having a hard time staying awake would benefit from having the option to stand instead of sit, or he may perhaps require accommodations such as receiving a copy of the notes after class. Remember to keep the IEP team informed about any concerns you may have. If side effects are severe, talk to the parent and IEP team about what you are seeing in your classroom—it is possible that the student can change the time of day he takes the medication, allowing him to be more alert when in your class, or that your classroom may not be an appropriate placement.

Social Skills

As we discussed in Chapter 1, social skills can be an area in which many students with disabilities stand out from their peers. In your classroom, this will often manifest as awkwardness in interactions with peers and with you, but it can include other classroom behaviors as well. In general, the student should have strategies he or she has learned to cope with social skill deficits, though your role may include reminding the student to use the strategies. For instance, the student may have a laminated card with reminders about working with peers, and you may want to refer the student to review the card before group work begins. It will also be helpful for you to give examples of appropriate and inappropriate behavior if you are going over behavioral expectations with the class. Also remember that you set the tone for your classroom, and other students' tolerance of their classmates' quirks may depend on how you react to situations in your classroom.

Classroom Disruptions

Many teachers have nightmares about that one student who causes major classroom disruptions in class every day. How a teacher defines "major" depends on context and can range from a few instances of calling out to a full-blown yelling-fest. As we have repeated many times, the IEP team would not suggest a student take your class if they did not believe the student could be successful, and that includes not having regular bouts of highly disruptive behavior. If your tolerance for interruption is very low, you may need to work on increasing your tolerance (see Figure 3.6). Snapping at students every time they are slightly disruptive ("I needed a tissue!") leads to more problems in the long run, including creating an unfriendly classroom environment.

FIGURE 3.6. INCREASING TOLERANCE FOR DISRUPTIVE BEHAVIOR

- Be aware of your tolerance, and question why your tolerance level is what it is. If there is a good reason (easily get headaches, safety during labs), communicate the reason for your high expectation to students.
- Remember that things that bother you don't necessarily have to disrupt the entire class. Consider covert ways to prompt a student back to task.
- Think about the function of the disruptive behavior and consider alternate ways for the student to fill the need, or provide the student with what he needs before he disrupts the class.
- Fake it. Someone's behavior might grate at your nerves, but you can pretend it doesn't; doing so will have the same outward effect as the behavior not bothering you at all.

"Argumentativeness"

It is a teenager's prerogative to disagree with adults, and some teenagers will disagree to the extreme at every opportunity, even if they do not have a disability. It is important that you try not to engage students once they get defensive if you know they will not take your explanation. For instance, on a bad day, a student with a mental health issue argues with you that the atomic number for oxygen is not eight; you, obviously, are right, but no matter what you say or show the student, she does not back down and continues to insist that you are wrong. At this point, it is best for you to back off, give the student time to process, and mentally reset. If you continue to engage with this student, or any student in such a defensive state, you will only waste time, energy, and the attention of the rest of your class.

In general, you can try to avoid some "argumentativeness" by explaining why you are asking students to do certain tasks (write out entire equations, not read the second half of the lab until everyone is done with the first, and so on). Providing clarity in your instructions will also help with this—the less wiggle room there is in your directions, the less a student can logically disagree ("You just said get out your book; you didn't say to open it!"). Finally, it is best to stay calm and not take the student's "argumentativeness" personally. Yes, he or she is arguing with you, but it's not about you. It may be about the student trying to push your buttons or gain control, but it is not an attack on you. Take deep breaths and redirect yourself and the student.

Excessive Questions

All kids go through a phase where they ask questions ad nauseam, but individuals with some disabilities, most typically Asperger's syndrome, continue this behavior. It is important to remember that the student cannot completely control this, and although it is natural for you to get frustrated, the better tact is to use strategies to help the student ask questions at appropriate times. Direct the student to write her questions down and ask at the end of class or during transition time. If the student is really struggling, you may consider limiting the number of questions she can ask by giving her five coupons and requiring that she turn in a coupon every time she asks a question. When the coupons are gone, she has to hold all questions. Over time this should help her determine which questions are most important and filter out superfluous questions.

Internalizing Disorders

Not all students with disabilities will exhibit behavior issues. Some of those who are not exhibiting overt, disruptive behaviors may have internalizing, or covert, behaviors that will affect their performance in your classroom. Anxiety and depression are examples of internalizing disorders that may manifest in a student pant in class all the same. You will know which students have this designation by reading student IEPs and talking to the case managers. You can glean information from these resources to help you know how best to approach the student in your classroom. Many students with anxiety will be working on learning or applying coping strategies, and if you can reinforce the use in your classroom, that will be helpful. For all students with internalizing disorder, it will be important for you to watch for any changes in behavior and immediately communicate those changes to the case manager and parents (Kauffman and Landrum 2009).

Working With Peers

Students with disabilities often have a difficult time making friends. If you have a socially awkward student in your class, consider their existing relationships as you assign groups. If the student is comfortable working with a particular peer, consider grouping those two together often, unless they are poor influences on each other. Individuals with disabilities often tend to socialize with individuals from whom they may not learn appropriate behaviors but instead who engage in risk behaviors and have behavioral issues themselves (Farmer et al. 2011). When you allow students to choose their own groups, keep an eye on how students interact with each other. Is there a student who is always picked last, with peers reluctant to let him or her in their group? If so, you may need to always assign groups so that peers do not have an opportunity to shun the student.

Cheating and Plagiarism

Though cheating is a concern for all teachers, there is no reason to believe students with disabilities are more likely than students without disabilities to cheat. Thus, you should approach any student with a disability you suspect of cheating or plagiarism in the same way you would approach a student without a disability. Begin the school year by being clear about what constitutes cheating and plagiarism in your classroom: Is it okay to have a parent give the student feedback on a paper? When students collaborate, how will work be divided? What are the guidelines for citing where the students get information?

If there is cheating and plagiarism in your classroom, it may be masking a greater problem, such as a student's inability to do the required work, or a student's lack of belief that they can do the work (McTigue and Liew 2011). Talk to the student about the issue to determine if this is a self-esteem issue, an improper placement, a lack of understanding expectations, or just pure and simple inappropriate behavior. It may be helpful to include the special education case manager in the discussion with students with disabilities, as the case manager may be aware of patterns of behavior.

It is also important to remember that accommodations are *not* cheating, though it is important for you to be clear with yourself, the IEP team, and the student about where the line is between using an accommodation and cheating. For instance, perhaps a student is allowed the accommodation of word processing his final exam essay questions. Does this include using spell check and grammar check? When you get the list of a student's accommodations at the beginning of the year, seek clarification on any items that concern you.

Discipline

Given the academically advanced nature of the students in your advanced science classes, and given that an IEP team has decided that any student with a disability in your class will be able to successfully complete the course, it is unlikely, yet possible, that students in your class will require high levels of discipline. It is important for you to understand what makes school-level discipline for a student with a disability different than for students without disabilities, so that you can understand that two students committing the same infraction and receiving different punishments is not a lack of justice; rather, it may be a difference in needs.

Students with disabilities who engage in behavior that would typically result in suspension, or temporary removal from school, may be suspended for as many as 10 days total during the school year without the IEP team needing to take any action. So, let's say that Phillip brings drugs to school—he can be suspended just as his peers without disabilities would be. However, before suspending Phillip for day 11 (for the same infraction or a series of different infractions), the IEP team must meet for what is called a manifestation determination hearing to determine if the behavior that caused the suspension is a result of Phillip's disability. The idea is that if the disability caused the behavior, then the IEP failed to meet Phillip's needs and we need to change the IEP. If the disability did not cause the behavior, then the IEP is accommodating the disability as it should be and the student should be suspended as the behavior would typically warrant (Bateman and Linden 2006). So, if the drugs Phillip brought to school were his bipolar medications, and he failed to drop them off with the school nurse because he was in a manic stage of his disorder, the infraction was directly related to his disability. The IEP team would meet, determine that the behavior was a manifestation of the disability, and consider adjustments to his behavior plan to prevent this behavior from happening in the future. If the team determines the behavior was not a result of the disability (perhaps Phillip brought marijuana to school), then Phillip would be suspended and the IEP team would not have to consider any IEP changes. So, students with disabilities can receive the same discipline that their nondisabled peers receive, depending on the circumstances.

Conclusion

Behavior management is probably never an issue in your advanced-level science class, and you should not assume that it will be now that you have a student with a disability in your class. Remember that good preparation on your part will go a long way toward creating an environment in which the student has no reason to engage in major misbehaviors. Having knowledge of consequences and strategies already in place creates consistency so the student avoids changes in rules or expectations between your classroom and other settings. Finally, if you do have concerns or any issues arise, remember that the special education teacher is your best resource.

IDEAS TO GET YOU STARTED

- Review your current classroom management practices. Are your expectations clear? Do you have smooth transitions?
- Review any BIPs in your student's IEP. Do you understand the behavior and what to do if the student exhibits the behavior in your classroom? If not, talk to the special educator to get clarification.
- Does one of your current students need a behavior contract? Think about how to negotiate a deal with him or her to improve behavior.

References

Bateman, B. D., and M. A. Linden. 2006. *Better IEPs: How to develop legally correct and educationally useful programs.* 4th ed. Verona, WI: Attainment.

Cook, M. N. 2005. The disruptive or ADHD child: What to do when kids won't sit still and be quiet. *Focus on Exceptional Children* 37 (7): 1–8.

Farmer, T. W., M. Leung, M. P. Weiss, M. J. Irvin, J. L. Meece, and B. C. Hutchins. 2011. Social network placement of rural secondary students with disabilities: Affiliation and centrality. *Exceptional Children* 78: 24–38.

Graham-Day, K. J., R. Gardner, and Y. Hsin. 2010. Increasing on-task behaviors of high school students with attention deficit hyperactivity disorder: Is it enough? *Education & Treatment of Children* 33: 205–221.

Gregory, A., and M. B. Ripski. 2008. Adolescent trust in teachers: Implications for behavior in the high school classroom. *School Psychology Review* 37: 337–353.

Hendley, S. L. 2007. 20 ways to use positive behavior support for inclusion in the general education classroom. *Intervention in School and Clinic* 42: 225–228.

Kauffman, J. K., and T. J. Landrum. 2009. *Characteristics of emotional and behavioral disorders of children and youth.* 9th ed. New York: Merrill Education/Prentice Hall.

McTigue, E., and J. Liew. 2011. Principles and practices for building academic self-efficacy in middle grades language arts classrooms. *The Clearing House* 84: 114–118.

Rafferty, L. A. 2010. Step-by-step: Teaching students to self-monitor. *Teaching Exceptional Children* 43 (2): 50–58.

Scott, T. M., P. J. Alter, and K. McQuillan. 2010. Functional behavior assessment in classroom settings: Scaling down to scale up. *Intervention in School and Clinic* 46: 87–94.

Solar, E. 2011. Prove them wrong: Be there for secondary students with an emotional or behavioral disability. *Teaching Exceptional Children* 44 (1): 40–45.

CHAPTER 4

Classroom Considerations: Instruction

The previous chapters have presented an overview of special education laws, definitions of key terms, and an introduction to the IEP and behavior concerns. This chapter will focus on your classroom. When students with disabilities are part of your advanced, honors, or accelerated classroom (to be referred to as *advanced class*), the content (curriculum) of the class will remain the same. However, you may need to make some slight adjustments to your instruction to ensure that all of your students are successful. As an experienced science teacher, you are familiar with the curriculum and know how to engage your students, manage your classroom, and assess student learning. These skills will serve as an excellent foundation for including students with disabilities.

One of the premises of instruction in the advanced classroom is the in-depth knowledge of scientific concepts and processes (discipline knowledge) by the science teacher. You know the science content. Additionally, you must also be conversant with concepts of learning, as they are the foundation of your instruction. In fact, the National Research Council (NRC 2002) has defined seven principles of learning that are important for the advanced study of math and science. Please see Figure 4.1 (p. 46) for a list of these principles.

These principles provide a foundation for instruction in the advanced science classroom. For example, Principle 1 addresses how learning is enhanced by using prior knowledge and focusing on major concepts in the discipline. In an honors biology course, the basic structure of a cell becomes a "building block" or foundation knowledge for concepts related to heredity, genetics, photosynthesis, and evolution. When including students with disabilities, the course still addresses these concepts, and graphic or advanced organizers can support learning as outlined in the fourth principle. Consider how students could label a drawing of cell or how they can use a Venn diagram to illustrate genetic concepts. You may already do this in your classroom.

FIGURE 4.1. SEVEN PRINCIPLES OF LEARNING

Here are the National Research Council's (2002) seven principles of learning:

- Learning with understanding is facilitated when new and existing knowledge is structured around the major concepts and principles of the discipline.
- Learners use what they already know to construct new understandings.
- Learning is facilitated through the use of metacognitive strategies that identify, monitor, and regulate cognitive processes.
- Learners have different strategies, approaches, patterns of abilities, and learning styles that are a function of the interaction between their heredity and their prior experiences.
- Learners' motivation to learn and sense of self affects what is learned, how much is learned, and how much effort will be put into the learning process.
- The practices and activities in which people engage while learning shape what is learned.
- Learning is enhanced through socially supported interactions.

Source: NRC 2002, p. 119.

As you read through the following discussion of instructional methods, progress monitoring, effective strategies, accommodations, and grading, you should note suggestions that you can incorporate into your own teaching practice. You may also find that you are already using many of these ideas, or you may have an idea that will work for a particular student in your classroom.

Inquiry-Based Methods

In addition to the seven principles of learning, the National Research Council (2002) also discusses the importance of using inquiry-based approaches in the advanced classroom. Inquiry-based approaches encourage students to learn the "process of science," which is an important conceptual framework for all disciplines of science. Inquiry-based approaches historically have been part of the science curriculum because the "scientific method" promotes this approach. In 1996, inquiry-based methods were standardized for the K–12 curriculum in the form of the *National Science Education Standards* (NRC 1996). The document encompassing the standards defines inquiry as a student process of

> making observations; posing questions; examining books and other sources of information to see what is already known; planning investigations; reviewing what is already known in light of experimental

> evidence; using tools to gather, analyze, and interpret data; proposing answers, explanations, and predictions; and communicating the results. (NRC 1996, p. 23)

How you use inquiry-based methods in your science classroom depends on the discipline (e.g., biology, physics), scientific concepts (Newton's laws of motion) addressed in the curriculum, and your own instructional style. Another issue that can arise when including students with disabilities in your classroom is how much teacher support or scaffolding you will provide as students investigate science concepts. Some science teachers use an inquiry-based approach with very little guidance so that the students must construct their own questions as they explore the scientific concept under discussion. Students have resources and materials (textbooks, web-based resources, and equipment for experiments) but then actively explore the concept on their own or with a partner. This process encourages students to develop both inductive and deductive reasoning skills. Remember, deductive reasoning has students using generalizations to build concepts ("If A is true, then B follows" statements), while inductive reasoning has students using specific observations to make more generalized statements or to describe principles (Glasgow, Cheyne, and Yerrick 2010). Although this is an instructionally sound method, it can be very frustrating for students whose disability impedes generalization skills, such as those on the autism spectrum.

"Guided" Inquiry-Based Approaches

Some inquiry-based approaches provide students with more scaffolding through the use of guided questions, lab instructions, and coaching. Students still actively explore the concepts but are "guided" through their explorations with teacher support. Both inquiry-based approaches encourage students to use their explorations to construct their knowledge of the concept; however, for many students with disabilities, the teacher-supported version is more successful (Scruggs and Mastropieri 2007). Consider the example of building a parachute for an egg drop in physics. Teachers could provide very little support by simply posing the task, in a more intense inquiry approach, or teachers could provide students with background questions to guide students toward thinking about the different ways to approach the project (e.g., slowing the rate at which the egg drops, dispersing the energy). Depending on the curriculum and the individual needs of students, teachers provide various levels of scaffolding. Recently, there has been an increased focus on independent research by students in these classrooms, and teachers should consider incorporating more guidance at the beginning of the school year with lessening support through the school year using inquiry-based approaches.

Argument Construction

Another way to incorporate an inquiry-based approach is to have students create an argument around a scientific concept or principle (Sampson and Grooms 2010). Students work in groups of three or four to review available data, theories, or laws, then develop a conclusion, explanation, or other claim in an argument form, similar to debate preparation, to support their conclusions. The group then presents this to the class as a poster session or video (Linz, Heater, and Howard 2011). Having students work in small groups can be another way for students with disabilities to successfully engage in inquiry-based learning. Small-group projects and activities are also known as cooperative learning and will be further discussed in Chapter 5. The smaller group size can provide more support and one-on-one interactions for all of the students, including those with disabilities. Additionally, teachers can assign students specific roles in the debate preparation, easily adapting assignments for a student with disabilities (a student with a physical disability who cannot write well or a student with learning disabilities who does not write well under pressure could be assigned to edit the video on the computer).

Inquiry-Based Activities and Writing

Paul Jablon (2006) proposed using an inquiry-based approach to solidify writing skills. Students engage in inquiry learning activities (experiments, web research) and then begin to compose a written report. The writing process is structured through a series of steps and uses peer editing at several review points (Jablon 2006). The premise of this approach is that through inquiry-based activities, students can strengthen their written language skills by describing what happened. The strength of this model is that it addresses both an inquiry-based approach and writing development (a skill needed in the advanced classroom). Many students with disabilities struggle with writing, and this approach may be useful.

Summary

Inquiry-based approaches are vital to the teaching of science. After all, science is based on discovery and investigation. You may need to provide some additional scaffolding for students with disabilities, such as a worksheet with questions to prompt students' reasoning, a handout to visually represent linkages of key concepts, or individual coaching of students as concepts are discussed (Mastropieri and Scruggs 2010). Please see Figure 4.2 for some practical considerations when using this approach.

FIGURE 4.2. INQUIRY-BASED APPROACH: PRACTICAL CONSIDERATIONS

- *Classroom culture:* A successful inquiry-based approach allows for "trial and error" so multiple mistakes can happen as part of the process of exploring concepts. The classroom culture you foster must be accepting of mistakes and errors. Students with disabilities often hesitate to offer their opinion, make guesses, or try something new because they do not want to make a mistake or call attention to themselves. Strive to create a classroom where risk taking or making mistakes is not just acceptable but encouraged. For example, model following a method that is not correct, or including a section on lab sheets for methods that were tried but unsuccessful.
- *Physical environment:* In an inquiry-based approach, students must be able to move about the classroom, gather materials, and record data. Consider how you will manage "traffic flow" as students move to their workstations. Consider how difficult it may be for a student in a wheelchair to get to a workstation. For students with visual impairments, consider the lighting levels you need for specific experiments, viewing videos, or simply reading a stopwatch. For students with hearing impairments, consider ambient noise levels and position of equipment (such as fans), and speak clearly so students can hear directions.

  Some students with disabilities may be distracted by multiple posters or charts on the walls. Cluttered or disorganized classrooms can also distract students with learning disabilities. Students with emotional disabilities may be uncomfortable if forced to work with more than one person nearby. When setting up your classroom and lab spaces, consider the implications for all of your students. Strive to create a well-organized space that can support students' explorations.
- *Questioning and commenting style:* In an inquiry-based approach, it is important for the questions and comments to be supportive without providing an evaluation of the student's statements to encourage students to think about the concepts independently. This can be particularly challenging when including students with disabilities. Students with disabilities often seek verbal assurance or encouragement that they are asking or doing what is appropriate, so they may ask for evaluative statements that do not foster their own independent thought.

  It can also be difficult to provide this type of verbal feedback when the student is not correct in his statements or analysis. Remember, in an inquiry-based approach, students construct their own knowledge through questioning, experimenting, and analyzing. You need to be supportive of the students while not providing verbal evaluations of their process. Consider using some of the following types of statements suggested by Moroney, Finson, Beaver, and Jenson (2003, p. 21.):

    - "That is one variable to think about, are there any others?"
    - "That is one idea, can anybody think of any other ideas?"
    - "How could you test that idea?"
    - "What other ways could you test that?"

FIGURE 4.2 *(continued)*

- *Focus on thinking:* In an inquiry-based approach, assist students with focusing on their own thinking by incorporating metacognitive or "thinking" strategies. Help students question their own thinking by generating a list of questions about the concept, actively considering "what if" questions, and creating links between ideas by drawing concept maps (Mastropieri and Scruggs 2010). Many students with disabilities will have prior exposure to these types of strategies and should be encouraged to use them. Strive to have students become adept at talking through their thought processes as a way to focus on their thinking.

Progress Monitoring

Most teachers have a method to assess or measure on an ongoing basis what the students know about the material being taught. They often assess how students are progressing toward a goal (Spinelli 2006) through homework problems, exit slips, warm-up questions, or informal questioning during class discussions (Linz, Heater, and Howard 2011). This type of formative assessment is progress monitoring and is used to inform instruction and predict if students are on track to meet long-term goals. It provides teachers a snapshot of how the students are performing and also offers the opportunity to use data to adjust instruction (such as review vocabulary or reteach an equation) to help solidify student understanding (Potts and Howard 2011). See Figure 4.3 for more information on a specific progress monitoring tool, curriculum-based measurement (CBM).

This type of ongoing assessment will be crucial as you include students with disabilities in your classroom. For example, you may find that a student has difficulty converting units of measures (centimeters, meters per hour) when working equations. Or you may find that a student has difficulty writing a hypothesis statement on lab reports. You may find that a student is more successful when drawing a picture prior to working an equation. As you gain more information on individual students, you can anticipate areas or tasks that may be difficult for them. You can also develop handouts, prompts, graphic organizers, or other ways to help students succeed. Another important aspect of formative assessment is homework, which will be discussed later in this chapter.

FIGURE 4.3. PROGRESS MONITORING DATA COLLECTION USING CURRICULUM-BASED MEASUREMENT (CBM)

CBM is a progress-monitoring tool in which teachers develop ungraded mini-quizzes (or probes) that contain information from the entire curriculum, including both what you have already taught and what you have yet to teach. Students take probes frequently (once or twice a week) and scores are graphed, with a goal of getting all items correct by the end of the year, or when it is time to take the end-of-year assessment. Graphs should indicate a steady increase toward the goal, and if they do not, the teacher knows that something needs to change or students will not meet the long-term goal of, for instance, passing the AP exam (Deno 2003). With the advanced population, teachers will want to look at their instruction, but students may also track their own progress and reflect on their own studying and preparation behaviors.

Research Base

A great deal of research has repeatedly demonstrated that taking frequent measures of student progress toward mastering specific content and adjusting instruction based on the projection of the student's progress toward the long-term goal yields higher academic achievement than not using progress-monitoring measures (Stecker, Lembke, and Foegen 2008). Though the research has not been specific to secondary science classes, there is evidence that CBM probes have predictive validity for secondary students on end-of-course assessments in reading (Espin et al. 2010), social studies (Espin, Busch, and Shin 2001), and writing, though less than in other areas (Amato and Watkins 2011). Here are some CBM examples:

- *Chemistry:* Develop probes that contain a random sample of the element symbols and names. Students match the symbols to names, and they will name more of them correctly as they learn all of the elements.
- *Physics:* Develop probes that require students to produce and/or use formulas, and count each step or part of the process as one point when scoring. Be sure there are enough possible points and that problems have a range of difficulty so you will be able to see an increase in the number of points earned as students learn different types of processes.
- *Biology:* Develop probes that include key vocabulary from throughout the year. Each probe will have a sample of vocabulary, and as students learn more throughout the year, their performance on probes will improve. See Espin, Busch, and Shin (2001) for directions and pointers on how to do this.

CHAPTER 4

FOSTERING STUDENT INDEPENDENCE: TRACK YOUR OWN PROGRESS

Did you know there is a way for you to determine how well you are doing with your science class content before getting to the end-of-unit test? If your teacher does not use something similar, consider making yourself mini-quizzes with vocabulary, or other information you are memorizing, from the entire unit. Take the quizzes, with the information jumbled, twice a week, and graph how many you get right, with the goal of getting all items right by test time. If you see that your progress will not allow you to meet your goal, reflect on what you can do to learn the material better:

- Have I spent enough time studying?
- Have I been studying the right material in an effective way?
- Can I ask for more resources to better understand the material?
- Can I find a study partner to help reinforce concepts?

You can work with your special education case manager to set up your mini-quizzes and track your progress until you get the hang of it.

Instructional Strategies That Work

As an experienced teacher, you know what strategies are most effective for your lessons. As you include students with disabilities, you will find that some of your strategies may need to be slightly adjusted, or you may want to try a strategy you have not used before. These adjustments should be easy to do without disrupting your individual teaching. In fact, you may find that you are already using many of these strategies.

Another important component of the advanced classroom is that most of the learners are high-ability and/or high-achieving students. These students often are motivated by a desire to succeed and want to pursue a college degree after high school. The students with disabilities in your advanced classroom are also high ability and motivated; however, their disability may inhibit or affect classroom performance. You need to consider how to ensure that the student's IEP accommodations are followed in your class.

Recently, there has been a focus on using evidence-based instructional strategies that have been shown to be effective through research. The U.S. Department of Education's Institute of Education Sciences sponsors a clearinghouse with a website titled "What Works Clearinghouse" (*http://ies.ed.gov/ncee/wwc*) that provides excellent information on evidence-based strategies. Some evidence-based strategies include advanced or graphic organizers, mnemonics, and peer-assisted strategies (especially when working with lab partners, which will be discussed in the following chapter;

Forness, Kavale, Blum, and Lloyd 1997). These strategies are effective with all learners, including those with disabilities. You may already be using these strategies.

Using the most effective strategies for all learners is an underlying premise of Universal Design for Learning (UDL). In Chapter 1, UDL was discussed as the idea that by making our instruction work for most students, fewer changes will be needed for students with disabilities. As you read through the following sections, it should become clear that any student in an advanced classroom can use most of the strategies described. Therefore, choosing to use a strategy that differentiates your instruction to include students with disabilities does not diminish or limit your instructional choices. In fact, using these evidence-based strategies promotes classwide success.

There may be concerns with the reading of textbooks, note-taking, and how to follow required accommodations in your classroom. Again, the following discussion will provide strategies and suggestions that can be effective for all of your learners. Every student may not need all of these strategies, but this discussion is intended to help you pick and choose strategies that can assist students with minor adjustments to your instruction.

Advanced and Graphic Organizers

You may already provide the notes pages of a PowerPoint presentation as handouts for students, or you may provide a chart to be completed during experiments. These are examples of advanced or graphic organizers, which include study guides, flow charts, diagrams, and other visual ways in which to provide the information (Mastropieri and Scruggs 2010). You may be most familiar with interactive science notebooks, another type of graphic organizer.

Depending on the discipline (biology, physics) and the curricular goals, providing partially constructed diagrams or charts for students to complete can help solidify the comprehension of material. For example, when covering the topic of the rate constant for chemical equations, provide a chart that students can complete as they run various experiments and record the rates of the reaction, including units of measure. In a biology class, have students complete a diagram of a nerve cell by labeling all of the cell parts and showing how the cell transmits across a synapse.

The purpose of graphic organizers is to help promote understanding of concepts, show relationships between concepts, and make abstract concepts more concrete through the visual display of the information (Dexter, Park, and Hughes 2011). Graphic organizers can also be used to show links to prior knowledge, helping students see how concepts relate to each other. Teachers often create their own organizers (Microsoft SmartArt is a good resource), but you can also purchase organizers through publishers of textbooks and course materials or find them online for free. Many of the curriculum resources found at the College Board's Advanced Placement website include graphic organizers.

While graphic organizers can be an excellent instructional tool, it is important to consider the purpose for using them each time you choose to do so. For example, graphic organizers need to simplify and illustrate the important information. So, when discussing any concept that may have a hierarchal structure, it is most useful to use a similar organizer (like a pyramid shape) every time you show hierarchal relationships (Dexter, Park, and Hughes 2011). Additionally, do not distract from the important information by putting too much information on the organizer or making it visually "busy." It is also important to provide enough space so that students can write on the organizer. Please see Figure 4.4 for examples of basic shapes that can be used as graphic organizers. Consider how you can incorporate graphic organizers into your instruction or modify those that you already use.

Mnemonics

Mnemonics are memory strategies that help students remember content. Mnemonics are an effective strategy for students with disabilities to help them remember key words and concepts (Forness, Kavale, Blum, and Lloyd 1997). Additionally, mnemonics are an effective way for students with learning disabilities to learn science content (Therrien et al. 2011). Though the research we have cited refers to students with disabilities, a broader range of students will benefit from these memory strategies, especially when learning a great deal of information in a short time. Students who do not need the memory strategy, or who naturally make up their own, will not be harmed if you introduce a mnemonic to the class. Most science teachers are familiar with "**M**y **V**ery **E**fficient **M**other **J**ust **S**erved **U**s **N**achos" as a way to remember the planets (Mercury, Venus, Earth, Mars, Jupiter, Saturn, Uranus, and Neptune). Or you may know the mnemonic in biology to remember kingdom, phylum, class, order, family, genus, species as "**K**ing **P**hillip **C**ame **O**ver **F**or **G**reen **S**oup." You may know the acronym PEN, which stands for protons, electrons, and neutrons. All of these are ways to remember information. You may already use these tricks! A quick web-based search will reveal many others, and you can encourage students to create their own. Please see Figure 4.5 (p. 56) for information on the mnemonic P.I.E.S., which can be used to assist students in solving word problems. Again, all learners can use this strategy, and it can be particularly useful for providing a starting point for solving problems during examinations.

Textbooks

In the advanced classroom, reading to understand the content is vital to student success. Assigned reading in textbooks is a common instructional practice; how-

FIGURE 4.4. EXAMPLES OF GRAPHIC ORGANIZERS

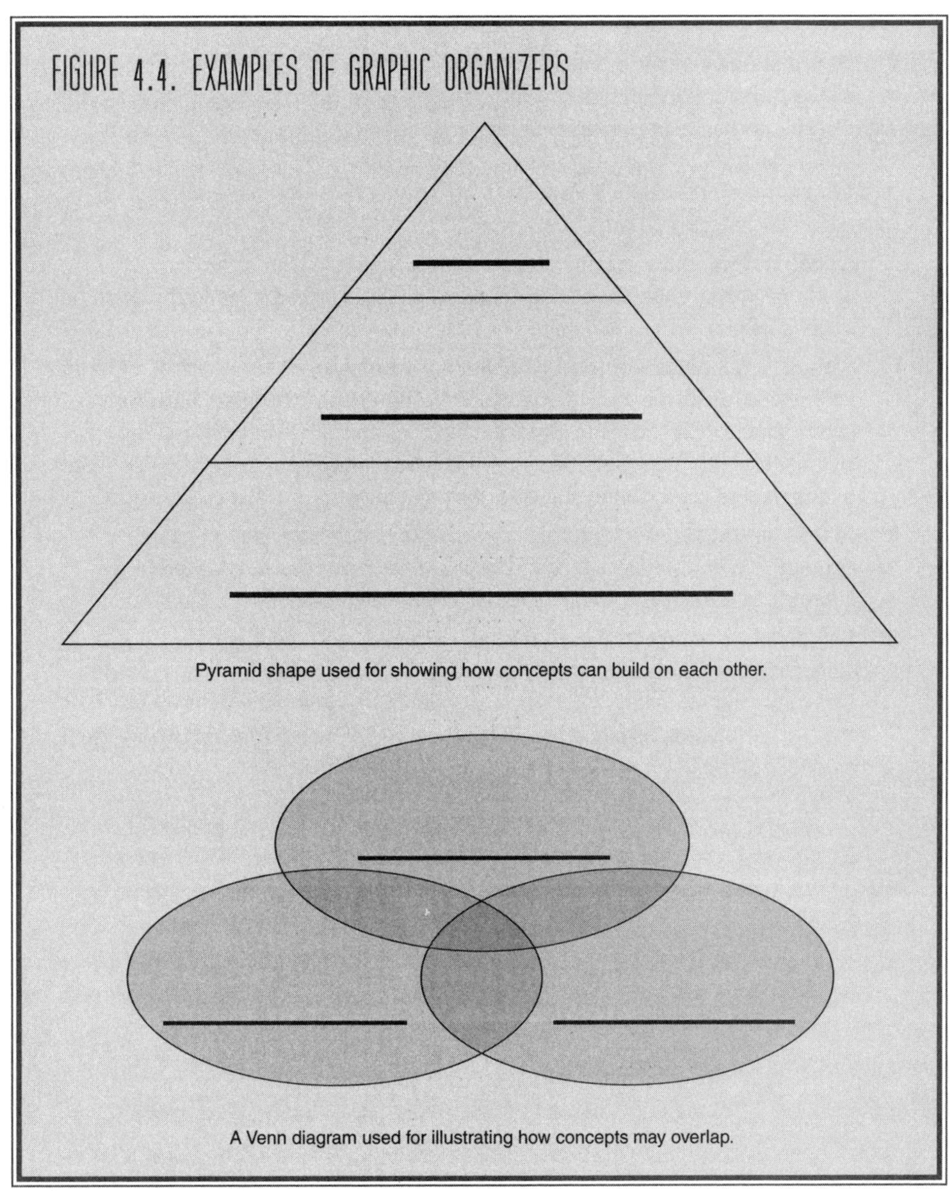

Pyramid shape used for showing how concepts can build on each other.

A Venn diagram used for illustrating how concepts may overlap.

ever, many students with disabilities may be reluctant or poor readers. Some students may have a learning disability related to reading (such as dyslexia) or poor reading comprehension skills. Some students may be quite proficient at solving equations or verbally explaining a concept, but have difficulty comprehending what they have read.

While it is not the purpose of an advanced science class to provide remedial reading instruction, there are a few strategies that can assist students with reading

FIGURE 4.5. P.I.E.S.: A STRATEGY FOR SOLVING WORD PROBLEMS

P.I.E.S. is a strategy intended to provide a systematic way to solve word problems. When faced with a story problem, many students will struggle with where to start. With P.I.E.S., the student has an immediate plan of action and can at least get started on the problem by making a visual representation of it. Just having a place to start can drive students on through the next steps and eventually to completion with a successfully solved problem.

P Stands for **P**icture. The student should draw a representation of the story. No art ability is required; in fact, we often demonstrate this part of the strategy with crude stick-figure pictures to show that the quality of the picture is not what matters.

I Stands for **I**nformation. The student should "mine" the word problem for important information (as in, dig through the words to find the gold nuggets) and identify what variable it belongs with. Students who find this difficult are encouraged to circle or highlight the keywords in the problem as they read it. The variable that is unknown should be identified with a question mark.

E Stands for **E**quation. The student is now able to search a menu of given equations to find which one can be used to solve the problem based on the information they have identified. He or she must write it down in equation form.

S Stands for **S**olve. When the information is identified and the equation is selected, the student inserts the information directly below the associated variable in the equation to solve the problem. Students must show every mathematical step, because this helps the teacher discover if and where the student has weak math skills. If the solution is incorrect, the teacher can find where the mistake was made. We also insist the student circle the answer to allow us to see her final solution—and for the student to express satisfaction at having solved a word problem!

Here's an example: Sam drove 45 mph from 1:30 p.m. until 3:30 p.m.. How far did he drive?

P

I $v = 45$ mph $t = 2$ hours $d = ?$

E $d = vt$ $d = 45\ (2)$

S **$d = 90$ miles**

When a story problem is given as an assessment, you can give points for the completion of each step. Such a problem could be worth 10 points, with 2 points for each step, 1 point for assigning the correct units, and 1 point for circling the answer. Students who would have been tempted to skip or guess at an answer for this kind of problem in a multiple-choice test are more likely to go for the points and make an effort to solve the problem.

Source: Linz, Heater, and Howard 2011. Used with permission.

assignments. For example, some textbooks are also available as books on tape or digitally, which means a student could listen to the book. There is software that will read digital print, making it possible for scans of any text to become readable. These technologies are often used by students with visual impairments but may also assist students with other disabilities. Please check with your special education department if you think this might be appropriate for a student in your class or if it is listed as an accommodation on the IEP. The special education department should be able to locate taped or digital copies of books for student use. There are other technological devices that will be discussed in Chapter 6 that should be considered as well.

For students with disabilities struggling to comprehend the textbook, the special education teacher or reading specialist should have recommendations or suggestions for you. They may also be able to assist the student in a small-group setting (basic skills class, tutoring) with developing their reading skills. If you can provide assigned readings ahead of time, the special education teacher may be able to assist the student in reading the material, using comprehension strategies, and making sure the student is prepared before class.

Figure 4.6 provides a couple of strategies that can be incorporated in your classroom for all learners. Please be advised that these strategies are most effective when practiced on a regular basis. (This is something to consider when incorporating them into your lessons and managing your instructional time.)

FIGURE 4.6. STRATEGIES FOR READING COMPREHENSION

RAP Strategy

R: Read a paragraph
A: Ask yourself, "What are the main ideas and details in this paragraph?"
P: Put the main ideas and details into your own words.
(Schumaker, Denton, and Deschler 1984)

Multipass Strategy

Students need to read the content (or chapter) three times:

- First time: to learn main ideas or themes
- Second time: to gain specific information
- Third time: to answer questions about the content (think end-of-chapter questions)

(Schumaker, Deschler, Alley, and Denton 1982)

Source: Linz, Heater, and Howard 2011.

Note-Taking

Note-taking is a study skill that all potential college students, including all of your students, need to develop. Integrate teaching this skill into your usual instruction by providing guided notes (PowerPoint slides) and outlines to be filled in, and by teaching students how to make their own structure by identifying key words or concepts (Mastropieri and Scruggs 2010) or modeling note-taking. You might find it difficult to work on note-taking, as many students in the advanced classroom may already have sufficient note-taking skills. If a student with a disability needs support with this (or other study skills), please ask the special education teacher for ideas or to assist the student individually.

Many high schools and some college programs are encouraging the use of a format for notes called Cornell Notes, which was developed by the Cornell University Learning Center. This note-taking system can be used with all learners and does promote success in college. Students take notes in the following manner (Cornell University Learning Center 2007):

- *Record:* Take notes in short sentences during the lecture.
- *Question:* After the class, create some questions about the notes. Consider linkages and meanings.
- *Recite:* Cover up the notes section and see if you can answer the questions in the cue or question column.
- *Reflect:* Ask yourself questions related to the notes, such as "Why is this important? How does it fit?"
- *Review:* Go over these notes on a weekly basis.

See Figure 4.7 for an example of Cornell Notes.

Some students with disabilities may not be physically able to write notes, and they should use a laptop or have the notes provided to them. Many schools use online course management systems or learning management systems such as Blackboard that offer students (and their parents) the opportunity to download notes and assignments. Prior to class, students can go to the Blackboard website and download the notes pages from the teacher's PowerPoint. This solution, where students independently download the notes pages, is a good option to provide the notes confidentially and for any student who may want to use them.

Another advance in technology that is becoming more accessible is the Smart Pen or Digital Pen. A Smart Pen contains a small recording device that can record the lecture while the student takes notes. By tapping the pen on the notes, the student can hear the lecture again. These are relatively inexpensive devices (cost is around $100) that can provide excellent note-taking support for students. There

FIGURE 4.7. CORNELL NOTES EXAMPLE

Divide an 8 ½ × 11 in. piece of notebook paper into three sections. Students are instructed to create every page of notes in this format and include their name, class, and date.

Student Name: ______________
Class: ______________
Date: ____________

2 ½ in.	6 in.
Cues or Key Words *You can also write questions in this column.* *<u>Carbon Dioxide</u>* *1st Element is Carbon* *Dioxide-Dio= 2 Oxygen (2 atoms)* CO_2 *<u>Nitrogen Trichloride</u>* *1st Element is Nitrogen*	**Take Notes in This Section** *<u>Naming Binary Covalent Compounds</u>* *Some rules about the names* *1. The first element is named first, using the name.* *2. Second element is named as an Anion (suffix "-ide")* *3. Prefixes are used to denote the number of atoms.* *4. "Mono" is not used to name the first element.* (College Board 2012)

Summary- *After class, summarize this page of notes here.*
There are rules for naming elements: 1st element is first, second element has "ide" and prefixes (di, tri) are used to tell the number of atoms.

FOSTERING STUDENT INDEPENDENCE: INSTRUCTIONAL STRATEGIES

Student, please ask yourself the following questions:

- Do I know what type of help I need for this assignment?
- Was I prepared for class today? (did the reading, did the homework, brought my notebook)
- Can I make a diagram or flow chart for this information?
- What's the best way for me to remember this information?
- Can I summarize the key points in the reading?
- Were there any new vocabulary words I should focus on knowing?
- If I didn't understand something in the discussion, can I follow up with the teacher later?
- Did I review my notes? Did they make sense to me?

is also a software program (IRIS notes) that allows users to take handwritten notes and make them into text through the use of a pen. There are also several "apps" for use with tablets that can assist in note-taking. While the use of these technological devices is encouraged, it should be noted that there is little research on their effectiveness for students with learning disabilities (Boyle 2012). Most likely this is related to the newness of the technology. You should experiment with different note-taking devices to find a helpful solution.

Of course, students can also use a small tape recorder to record lectures. All of these are helpful for students who are not adept at listening and writing at the same time and for those who are poor note-takers due to difficulties with identifying important information. Be creative in finding ways to help students take notes, since it is a skill that will support their success in college.

Accommodations

We discussed the definition of accommodations and provided some examples in Chapter 1, but you need to consider how you will include them during your instruction. It is important to remember that you do need to do them. They are not suggestions but legally required supports that must be done. Sometimes a teacher will disagree with a particular accommodation for a student (for example, reduced homework); however, whether you agree or disagree is not the issue. If the accommodation is listed on the student's IEP, it must be provided. Remember, IEPs are legal documents and an individual teacher may not change the IEP without the consent of the team (including the student's parents). This is actually a good reason to attend IEP meetings, so that you can offer your perspective as an advanced classroom teacher on what accommodations are appropriate. See Chapter 1 for some accommodation examples.

Some students with disabilities resist using their accommodations because they do not want to appear different than their peers. For example, a student may have extended test-taking time as an accommodation and may not use the extra time. Again, the accommodations are in place because the student needs the support; therefore, you should encourage students to use them. In fact, if you have an initial meeting with the student at the beginning of the school year, you could insist that he agree to use all of the stated accommodations.

Another approach is to use a learning contract that both you and the student sign that states he will use his accommodations as stated on the IEP. You might consider the learning contract as an opportunity for you and the student to discuss expectations for his attendance in your class. The contact could address issues of homework (he has to do it) and accommodations (he has to use them). It would be similar to the behavioral contracts discussed in earlier chapters. Please see Chapter 7 (p. 112) for an example of a learning contract.

For students in AP or IB classes, accommodations can become a significant issue with the end-of-the-year tests. Testing accommodations will be addressed as part of Chapter 7, but students should practice using their accommodations for tests. If a student continues to resist using the accommodations stated on her IEP, please contact the special education teacher for assistance. In rare cases, the IEP team may remove accommodations that a student does not want to use.

Another issue to consider when providing accommodations is how to provide them in a confidential manner. For example, you could provide notes pages to the entire class—not just the student with a disability. Or you could send a private e-mail with the number of homework problems reduced from 15 to 5. Once you begin thinking through what is needed for an individual student, you will be able to adjust so that the student's privacy is respected. Please see Figure 4.8 (p. 62) for more information on student confidentiality.

Grading and Tests

As an experienced teacher in the science classroom, you are well aware of how important homework, grading, and testing are to how your classroom functions. The role of homework is to help students practice the concepts they have explored during class and solidify their skills. Students (and their parents) are very concerned with grades and how to earn the highest marks. You probably prepare and administer tests on a regular basis. All of these instructional activities will continue when you have a student with a disability in your advanced class.

FIGURE 4.8. STUDENT CONFIDENTIALITY

No adolescent likes to be embarrassed, and this is also true for students with disabilities. Students with disabilities do not want to be treated differently than their peers. They often do not want their peers to know they have a disability. In some cases, the disability may be obvious—the student uses a wheelchair or has a hearing aid—but in other cases, there may be no outward sign of a disability. Recognize that an IEP is a confidential and legal document. Try to identify discreet ways to provide support to the student (for example, by providing a graphic organizer to the entire class or reducing the number of homework problems through an e-mail to the student).

Additionally, the Family Education Rights and Privacy Act (FERPA) is federal legislation that protects the privacy rights of students and their families. This is for all students, not just those with disabilities. For more information on FERPA, please review the Department of Education's website (*http://www2.ed.gov/policy/gen/guid/fpco/ferpa/index.html*).

FOSTERING STUDENT INDEPENDENCE: USING ACCOMMODATIONS

Student, please consider the following questions:

- Do I know what accommodations are on my IEP?
- Can I discreetly ask a teacher for an accommodation?
- I don't want to use an accommodation. Who should I tell?
- I need an accommodation that isn't on my IEP. How do I ask for it?

Homework

Students with disabilities frequently have "reduced homework" listed as an accommodation on their IEP. Sometimes teachers interpret to mean that students with disabilities should not have to do homework. This is not true! You should assign them homework, but the amount needs to be limited. For example, you may assign 15 physics problems at the end of a chapter in the textbook. For the student with the reduced homework accommodation, you need to reduce the number of homework problems to be completed. Perhaps you will have the student complete 6 problems instead. This can be a little time consuming because you will need to choose which problems the student should complete so that you can ascertain how well the student understands the concepts illustrated by the problems. It is easiest (and tempting) to just have the student do the first 6, but it is best to look at the skill practiced in each problem to determine which problems are the most critical. Students do not require reduced homework because they are incapable of exhibiting the skill or content; they require reduced homework because their disability affects their stamina, the amount of time it takes to complete tasks, or their emotional state when asked to do a task repeatedly.

Many students grumble or complain about completing homework; however, in the advanced classroom, most students are motivated to finish the assignments. However, some students who are "twice exceptional" or have a disability related to social deficits (such as Asperger's syndrome) may refuse to do the homework or show work on the assigned problems. They may insist the homework is "busy work." In many cases, the students can easily solve the assigned homework problems and do not see any benefit to completing the homework. This can be a difficult situation to manage. Compounding this difficulty is that these students often can easily earn high marks (96% or better) on unit tests, as they do comprehend the concept being taught.

Should this situation occur in your classroom, consider negotiating with the student the number of homework problems she needs to complete. You may want to remind the student that the course is a college-prep course, and learning to be disciplined about completing homework is an important skill for college. You may want to ask the special education teacher, the student's case manager, or a guidance counselor to also attend a meeting where you and the student negotiate homework. The student should complete some (reduced number of) homework problems on a regular basis to learn the skill of completing homework. Again, if you have had an initial meeting with the student at the start of the year, you can set homework expectations. This is another item to address on a learning contract signed at the beginning of the school year. (See Chapter 7, p. 112.)

Many teachers encourage homework completion by assigning grade points for completed homework. For the situation where students refuse to do the homework, providing points may not be motivating. The student may find herself getting high marks (A) on unit tests, but having course grades much lower (C) because she will not turn in any homework . This can become a challenging situation when an angry parent contacts you wanting to know how (or why) his student is doing poorly in your class when the test grades show the student to be knowledgeable about the content. Clearly stated grading policies will help alleviate this situation, but it is also helpful to keep the parents informed about the lack of homework completion early in the school year and talk to the special education teacher for more ideas.

Another issue to consider regarding homework is having students show their work. You probably require this so that you can identify areas of weakness and see how well students are grasping a particular concept. Some students with disabilities may have difficulty with this process. Students with physical disabilities may have poor handwriting; they may be encouraged to complete their homework on a laptop. Some students (often the "twice exceptional") resist showing their work because they "know the answer" by simply reading the problem. Their attitude is, "Why show work when the answer is so simple?" Again, you may want to negotiate with the student to show his work on some problems. You might remind him that showing his work on homework is a required skill for college. Other students with learning disabilities may become distracted and disorganized when showing work on multistep equations. Using the process steps described in Figure 4.5 (P.I.E.S.) may assist the student by providing a structure to show his work. As you get to know individual students, you will become confident in knowing how to approach the issue of showing work.

Finally, it is important to address the student who may have additional help at home with his assignments. Parents often become so invested in their student's success that they "overhelp" with homework. While this can happen with any parent, parents of students with disabilities have often been involved in the student's school achievement from an early age. These parents are used to monitoring and helping with homework. Should you suspect that this is happening, please contact the special education teacher and ask for assistance. Parents of students with disabilities have frequent communication with the special education teacher. The special education teacher may be able to provide insight and gently remind parents that students need to complete their homework independently. Some teachers in the advanced classroom establish rules about parental participation at the beginning of the school year through a letter addressed to parents. If this is your practice, make sure to send the letter home with all of your students (including those with disabilities).

Tests

As previously discussed, students with disabilities may have testing accommodations listed on their IEPs. While a student may need extended time to finish the test, the content of the test does not need changing. So, in most cases, you can use the same test for all of your students without making substantial changes to the content of the questions. If you have a student with a visual impairment, you may need to increase the font size of the test questions or arrange for the questions to be given orally. There are computer programs that can read the test aloud to the student. Similarly, if you have a student with a physical disability that limits her ability to hold a pencil, you may administer the same test but allow the student to use a laptop or other assistive device. These accommodations are intended to assist or support the student with the disability, not to change the content of the test. Remember, students should use their testing accommodations, and if they are reluctant to do so, please contact the special education teacher.

However, an issue you should consider is the test-taking skills of students. Many students with disabilities are poor test-takers and require explicit instruction on how to take tests (Mastropieri and Scruggs 2010). For courses that have high-stakes end-of-the-year examinations (such as AP exams), test-taking skills should be a focus of instruction early in the school year. These skills need to be practiced. All students can benefit from weekly practice on test-taking skills, so you should plan to build this practice into your instruction.

For some students, the act of taking a test provokes feelings of anxiety. This can be an issue for students with disabilities and their nondisabled peers. For students with emotional disabilities, this may require additional support from a school or guidance counselor to help students develop individual coping skills, as increased anxiety can affect overall classroom behavior. Please contact the special education teacher or school or guidance counselor should this become an issue with a particular student in your classroom. For other students, discussion and preparation for what happens during the test can be reassuring. This might include a discussion of breathing and the importance of breakfast and preparation for a test by practicing test-taking skills.

For teachers of AP science classes, the College Board at the AP course website (*http://apcentral.collegeboard.com/apc/Pageflows/TeachersResource/TeachersResourceController.jpf*) provides sample test questions from the end-of-the-year exam. These released test items are excellent questions to use as test-taking practice questions. Again, you should begin practice early in the school year, and it is most effective when practiced regularly (weekly). Figure 4.9 (p. 66) provides helpful hints on incorporating test-taking skills into your instruction. Further discussion of testing accommodations and end-of-year high-stakes tests will be provided in Chapter 7.

Grading

Teachers feel very strongly about their individual grading practices. Each teacher establishes policies based on his individual philosophy toward grading and what he thinks is important. For example, some teachers require all writing to be grammatically correct, and some will not accept late assignments; some only award points for a correct answer, while others will provide partial credit (or points) for the steps in the equation. The purpose of this discussion is not to debate your individual grading practice but to offer some suggestions that will assist you when including students with disabilities in your classroom.

First, your grading policies should be explicitly stated verbally and in writing (you may already do this). Students (and their parents) need to know what your expectations are for homework, tests, labs, and other assignments. For example, if homework problems with equations require that the final answer include

FIGURE 4.9. TEST-TAKING SKILLS

Students can be provided two sample test questions on a weekly basis. Give students 5 minutes to complete each problem. The teacher should then go over the answers while asking the students how they selected their answers. Try to keep this type of lesson to 20 minutes—it can be a very quick warmup at the beginning of the class period. Have students focus on the following:

Reading and Comprehending the Question

- Have students circle, underline, or box key words such as *compare, contrast*, and *not.*
- Have students identify (and mark) key vocabulary words such as *accelerate*, *time*, *distance, reaction rate*, and *genus*.
- Have students determine if the question is a word problem. If it is word problem, can they identify what strategy to use? (P.I.E.S., Figure 4.5)

Answering the Question

- *Multiple choice:* Can you identify or select the correct answer? Can you eliminate any answers that you know are not correct ("slash the trash")? When should you guess?
- *Word problems:* Can you follow the steps in P.I.E.S.? (Draw a *picture*, mine for *information*, find an *equation*, and *solve* the equation.)
- *Short essay:* Have the student practice writing out an answer.
- *Sketches or graphs:* Practice reading and interpreting graphs. Have students label illustrations. Have them practice drawing their own pictures and labeling them.

Providing Their Answers

- *Bubble sheets:* While these are becoming less prevalent, students may need to know how to complete one.
- *Computer programs:* Many high-stakes tests are being conducted on computers. Students need to know how to take the test on the computer. Have students practice for these types of tests on their laptop or at computer stations.

Source: Linz, Heater, and Howard 2011.

units of measurement, make sure you state this need. Or, if you do not accept late homework, this should be clearly written and emphasized. Some students with disabilities may need prompting to turn in homework. Others may have an accommodation for extended time on homework, which can be interpreted as the ability to turn homework in late. In this situation, make sure that the students and their parents understand what is acceptable to you. If you have questions about the intention of a homework accommodation, talk to the special education teacher.

A related issue is transparency in your expectations when grading projects, homework, and lab reports. Students need to know what is expected of them and how the project will be graded. For example, will students be penalized if their spelling of a chemical term is incorrect? Will they lose all of the points on a problem if they have a number reversal in a data listing? This concern is often addressed through the use of rubrics, which you may already use. Rubrics provide the opportunity to clearly define what is expected and how an assignment will be graded (Wiggins 1998).

Many of the College Board's Advanced Placement (AP) curriculum guides include sample grading rubrics. These can be found on the AP website that was noted in the previous section on released test items. There is also a link at this site to teacher discussion boards where materials (such as rubrics and labs) are shared. These can be excellent resources for locating sample rubrics that can be adapted for use in your classroom.

Please make sure to go over the rubric in class and present a written rubric that the students can review prior to submitting assignments for grading, as this will assist all of the students. Many students with disabilities are familiar with using rubrics. In fact, they may expect to have a modified rubric used. For students in your advanced classroom, modified rubrics should rarely be needed. These students are capable of performing at a level with their nondisabled peers; therefore, they should not need any modifications to curriculum. Occasionally, there may be a specific accommodation (reduced writing) that you will need to adapt a rubric to accommodate. For example, a lab report may require students to write a three- or four-paragraph conclusion to earn full credit. The student with the reduced writing accommodation may earn full credit for writing one or two paragraphs. Once you are familiar with the IEP accommodations for the students in your class, any needed adaption on a rubric should be quite easy to accomplish.

Finally, another issue to discuss is the importance of grading standards. As you are aware, the standards you maintain in your grading reflect the advanced nature of the course. In fact, AP courses are to be graded as though they are college-level courses. The students with disabilities placed in your class can perform to the same standard as their nondisabled peers. In other words, you should not modify your expectations or the standard of work you require for these students. The performance standards for students with disabilities should be the same as other students, but keep in mind that they may need a little extra support (accommodations) to perform at the set standard.

Conclusion

This chapter has provided a discussion of strategies (mnemonics, graphic organizers), accommodations, homework, tests, and grading. All of these classroom considerations are important to how you provide instruction in your advanced classroom. You should be reassured that including students with disabilities will require only minor adjustments to your instruction. Including students with disabilities can provide opportunities to "fine tune" your instruction and try new ways of doing things. We encourage you to embrace these challenges and enjoy the adventure!

IDEAS TO GET YOU STARTED

- At the beginning of the school year, review your lesson and unit plans to identify any potential areas of difficulty for students with disabilities.
- Seek assistance from the special education teacher.
- Review your class syllabus to make sure your grading policies are clearly stated.
- Consider your letter home to parents a way to communicate your expectations (homework and grading policies).
- Identify and review resources on including students with disabilities in your classroom. (Remember, the College Board has a website that will help for AP classes.)
- Throughout the school year, review (or create) mnemonics to help all students remember important information.
- Review or create graphic organizers to use as handouts. Remember that many of these are available through course materials and in the curriculum guides posted on the AP website.
- Identify any needed accommodations and make notes on how you will address them.
- Consider using a learning contract (see example on p. 112).

References

Amato, J. M., and M. W. Watkins. 2011. The predictive validity of CBM writing indices for eighth-grade students. *Journal of Special Education* 44: 195–204.

Boyle, J. R. 2012. Note-taking and secondary students with learning disabilities: Challenges and solutions. *Learning Disabilities Research & Practice* 27 (2): 90–101.

College Board. 2012. *AP chemistry teacher's guide. http://apcentral.collegeboard.com/apc/public/courses/teachers_corner/2119.html*

Cornell University Learning Center. 2007. *Cornell notes. http://lsc.sas.cornell.edu/Sidebars/Study_Skills_Resources/cornellsystem.pdf*

Deno, S. L. 2003. *Developments in curriculum-based measurement. Journal of Special Education* 37: 184–192.

Dexter, D. D., Y. J. Park, and C. A. Hughes. 2011. A meta-analytic review of graphic organizers and science instruction for adolescents with learning disabilities: Implications for the intermediate and secondary science classroom. *Learning Disabilities Research & Practice* 26 (4): 204–213.

Espin, C. A., T. W. Busch, and J. Shin. 2001. Curriculum-based measurements in the content areas: Validity of vocabulary-matching as an indicator of performance in social studies. *Learning Disabilities Research & Practice* 16: 142–152.

Espin, C., T. Wallace, E. Lembke, H. Campbell, and J. D. Long. 2010. Creating a progress-monitoring system in reading for middle-school students: Tracking progress towards meeting high-stakes standards. *Learning Disabilities Research & Practice* 25: 60–75.

Forness, S. R., K. A. Kavale, I. M. Blum, and J. W. Lloyd. 1997. Mega-analysis of meta-analyses: What works in special education and related services. *TEACHING Exceptional Children* 29 (6): 4–9.

Glasgow, N. A., M. Cheyne, and R. K. Yerrick. 2010. *What successful science teachers do: 75 research-based strategies.* Thousand Oaks, CA: Corwin Press.

Hallahan, D. P., J. M. Kauffman, and P. C. Pullen. 2009. *Exceptional learners: An introduction to special education.* 11th ed. New York: Allyn & Bacon, Pearson Education.

Jablon, P. 2006. Writing through inquiry. *Science Scope*. April/May: 18–20.

Linz, E., M. J. Heater, and L. A. Howard. 2011. *Team teaching science: Success for all learners*. Arlington, VA: National Science Teachers Association.

Mastropieri, M. A., and T. E. Scruggs. 2010. *The inclusive classroom: Strategies for effective instruction.* 4th ed. Upper Saddle River, NJ: Pearson.

Moroney, S. A., K. D. Finson, J. B. Beaver, and M. M. Jensen. 2003. Preparing for successful inquiry in inclusive science classrooms. *TEACHING Exceptional Children* 36 (1): 18–25.

National Research Council (NRC). 1996. *National science education standards*. Washington, DC: National Academies Press.

National Research Council (NRC). 2002. *Learning and understanding: Improving advanced study of mathematics and science in U.S. high schools.* Committee on Programs for Advanced Study of Mathematics and Science in American High Schools. J. P. Gollub, M. W. Bertenthal, J. B. Labov, and P. C. Curtis, eds. Center for Education, Division of Behavioral and Social Science and Education. Washington, DC: National Academies Press.

Potts, E. A., and L. A. Howard. 2011. *How to co-teach: A guide for general and special educators*. Baltimore, MD: Brookes Publishing.

Sampson, V., and J. Grooms. 2010. Generate an argument: An instructional model. *The Science Teacher* 77 (6): 32–37.

Schumaker, J. B., P. H. Denton, and D. D. Deschler. 1984. *Learning strategies curriculum: The paraphrasing strategy*. Lawrence: University of Kansas.

Schumaker, J. B., D. D. Deschler, G. R. Alley, and P. H. Denton. 1982. Multipass: A learning strategy for improving reading comprehension. *Learning Disability Quarterly* 5 (3): 295–304.

Scruggs, T., and M. Mastropieri. 2007. Science learning in special education: The case for constructed versus instructed learning. *Exceptionality* 15 (2): 57–74.

Spinelli, C. G. 2006. *Classroom assessment for students in special and general education.* 2nd ed. Upper Saddle River, NJ: Pearson.

Stecker, P. M., Lembke, E. S., and Foegen, A. 2008. Using progress-monitoring data to improve instructional decision making. *Preventing School Failure* 52 (2): 48–58.

Therrien, W. J., J. C.Taylor, J. L.Hosp, E. R. Kaldenberg, and J. Gorsh. 2011. Science instruction for students with learning disabilities: A meta-analysis. *Learning Disabilities Research & Practice* 26 (4): 188–203.

Wiggins, G. 1998. *Educative assessment: Designing assessments to inform and improve student performance.* San Francisco, CA: Jossey-Bass.

CHAPTER 5

Labs

Laboratory experiments, hypothesis testing, data collection, and analysis are vital components of the advanced science classroom. Consider experiments using lasers in a physics class, creating chemical reactions during chemistry class, and using microscopes to identify plant cells during biology class—all of these types of labs are useful in understanding the content and learning how to become a scientist. More recently, there has been a focus on supporting students in conducting independent research. This offers the opportunity for students to design research answering their own questions on a science topic (NRC 2002).

The purpose of including laboratory experiments and activities is to encourage students to think analytically, conduct experiments, draw conclusions from experiments, evaluate findings, consider further areas of study and questions to be answered, and effectively communicate these findings and conclusions (College Entrance Examination Board 2001). Laboratory experiments are an essential component to the accelerated classroom and provide an interactive learning environment linking science concepts to "real world" observations. While the actual laboratory experiments or exercises will vary depending on the content or discipline, there are more general concerns that should be addressed, such as maintaining student safety, working with a lab partner, writing a lab report, attending field trips, and conducting independent research.

When students with disabilities are part of your classroom, these concerns are still present and you need to consider some slight alterations in how you plan, organize, and address these challenges. Please do not consider these alterations as barriers to your teaching, but as an opportunity to view your labs with a new perspective. If including students with disabilities in your accelerated classroom is new to you, please be assured that you will gain experience through problem-solving situations. It will become easier to provide successful lab experiences for all of your students this year and in the future.

Safety

During all labs, safety concerns are of primary importance to the science teacher. Students must be able to use the lab equipment, follow safety procedures, and know what to do in the event that something goes wrong (Roy 2010). Safety procedures and concerns often are one of the first areas covered at the beginning of the school year. Some teachers provide demonstrations on how to use laboratory equipment and have students practice using the equipment. Students also practice safety procedures and learn how to use safety equipment (goggles, fire extinguishers, and so on). Some science teachers even include safety questions on quizzes and exams throughout the school year. This focus should not be changed when a student with a disability is placed in your classroom.

Safety Contracts

Many science teachers have students read and sign a safety contract at the beginning of the school year. Both the teacher and the student retain copies. The purpose of this contract is to ensure that students are aware of safety policies and procedures, as well as to provide documentation that the teacher addressed these concerns. This contract can be provided with the course syllabus and reviewed in one of the first class meetings of the new school year. It may be appropriate to share the contract in advance or privately in a meeting with the student with disabilities and their special education case manager. Students with disabilities should adhere to the same safety policies and procedures as their nondisabled peers in your classroom, but may benefit from extra time to review policies and procedures or additional opportunities to practice safety procedures.

Safety and Students With Disabilities

You should review the student's IEP and note any specific areas of difficulty that may affect how the student can learn and follow safety procedures (Linz, Heater, and Howard 2011). For example, does the student have difficulty with fine motor skills that may make holding calipers and test tubes or using a fire extinguisher difficult? What about a student with a hearing impairment—will he be able to hear your safety procedural guidelines or warnings? Safety for all students should be your concern. Upon reviewing the IEP and speaking with the special education teacher, you may find "work-arounds" for students with disabilities.

For some students with disabilities, you may want to have a private meeting with the student and the special education teacher or case manager to address individual needs. This meeting may be most effective at the beginning of the school year or following the IEP meeting where the IEP team discusses and sets the student's class schedule. During this time, you can learn about what the student needs for academic success, but it is also an opportunity to impress upon the student the importance of following safety procedures. If you use a safety contract, you can provide it at this meeting. In any such meeting, the purpose should be for mutual problem solving related to safety concerns, not to exclude the student or inhibit his participation in classroom activities or labs.

Some teachers also send a copy of the safety contract home and have parents sign the contract to indicate that they understand the importance of the lab rules. You can also purchase a supply of safety contracts from lab equipment companies such as Flinn Scientific. A sample safety contract can be viewed at the Flinn website (*www.flinnsci.com/teacher-resources/safety/general-laboratory-safety/flinn-scientific's-ideal-student-safety-contract*). Students with disabilities should adhere to the same safety policies and procedures as their nondisabled peers in your classroom. Please see Figure 5.1 (p. 74) for another example of a safety contract.

There are some safety procedures that you may already use that can be tweaked when including students with disabilities. For example, you may provide both verbal and written procedural safety guidelines for all students (thus including the student with the hearing impairment). You may choose to designate specific safety leaders among the students who are responsible for helping all students (another way to help the student with fine motor issues while assisting the whole class and not singling out the student with the disability). Essentially, you can maintain the same standards for all students while including students with disabilities, thus ensuring your class maintains a safe environment.

Another way to focus on safety is to provide color-coded index cards (laminated, so you can reuse them) with safety procedures on them. An example might be how to use the eyewash station or a fire extinguisher. These can be given to each set of lab partners at the beginning of a lab with a brief verbal review. Or, if the lab experiment being conducted has unusual procedures or equipment, you could provide a laminated index card with safety "pointers" for using the special equipment or highlighting the change in procedures. The preceding discussion has focused on ways to incorporate safety procedures for the entire class; the following section will provide suggestions for students with disabilities.

Suggestions for Students With Physical Disabilities

Students with physical disabilities will need varying degrees of support depending on the specific nature of the disability and the requirements of the lab experiment. For example, a student with fine motor control issues may have difficulty putting on safety glasses or holding a test tube. A student who uses mobility aids (wheelchairs, crutches, etc.) may need extra space to move in the lab station. A student with a hearing impairment may have difficulty following verbal instructions during an experiment. Consider the following:

FIGURE 5.1. SAMPLE SAFETY CONTRACT

Biology Honors Safety Contract

By signing at the bottom of this contract, I agree to the following:

1. I have read the course syllabus and I will behave responsibly.
2. I may have a bottle of water in my backpack but I will not drink from it during labs.
3. I will wear lab coats and safety goggles to ensure lab safety. I will wear closed-toe shoes.
4. I will only use equipment or touch animals with the teacher's permission.
5. I will not open animal cages on my own or tease the animals.
6. I will carefully use sharp objects (scalpels, scissors).
7. I will follow the teacher's instructions.
8. I will use caution when using matches, Bunsen burners, hot plates, or fire.
9. I know how to use the lab fire extinguisher, fire alarm, eyewash station, and other safety equipment. (The teacher will demonstrate equipment use during first week of class, and there will be a safety quiz.)
10. I know and will follow evacuation procedures. I know where the classroom exits are located.

Student signature: ______________________________

Teacher signature: ______________________________

Copy to parent (date): ________________

Do you wear contacts? ________

Do you have any allergies? ____________

- *Placement of the student's work station:* In some cases (hearing impairment), a position closer to the front of the classroom or teacher's desk may be most appropriate; however, the student should not be singled out. In other cases, it may be better to have the work station located near an exit, or on an end to provide extra workspace. Consider the configuration of your classroom when assigning work stations.
- *Use of simulations:* Some experiments can be conducted via software. While this is not acceptable in all situations, there are some advantages to using simulations. The experiment can be conducted several times in short period of time, and variables can be changed without having to change the physical set up of the experiment. It may be easier for students with limited mobility or fine motor control to use a computer. Please see Chapter 6 on assistive technology for more details.

Suggestions for Students With Specific Learning Disabilities and ADHD

Students with specific learning disabilities may be distractible, lose focus, lack organization, and have difficulty recalling and following safety instructions. These students often have messy lab stations that can create hazardous conditions. Consider the following actions:

- *Assign an appropriate work station:* Again, the student should not be singled out, but an assigned work station near the front of the classroom may help reduce distractions.
- *Provide both written and verbal instructions:* Instructions providing step-by-step directions can be used as a handout. As students work through the lab, they can refer to the handout to ensure they are on track. Encourage the students to check off each step as they complete the lab to self-monitor their progress.
- *Focus on work station organization:* Depending on the nature of the experiment, have students maintain an organized lab space. One way to encourage this is to use the analogy of a chef who must have a *mise en place* before starting to cook. *Mise en place* means the chef has organized the materials (ingredients, bowls, and pans) at the beginning of cooking. Have students organize their lab materials before beginning the experiment.
- *Provide extra supervision when using hazardous or dangerous materials:* Students may become distracted when using fire or handling a live animal. Re-emphasize any safety concerns at the beginning of the lab.

Suggestions for Students With Social Deficits (Asperger's Syndrome, Emotional Disabilities)

Students with emotional disabilities or Asperger's syndrome often have inappropriate social behavior. While this may not have a direct impact on lab safety, you should be aware that students with these types of disabilities may be disruptive at any time. This disruptiveness can include "argumentativeness" and difficulty transitioning to new activities. So, given that the student could disrupt the lab, please reiterate to all students the importance of safety at all times. If your student has a behavior plan, talk with the special educator about building in additional incentives for appropriate behavior and attention to safety during lab time or additional consequences for inappropriate behavior.

Support for Labs

In some situations, you may want to have a meeting with the IEP team or the case manager to discuss your concerns. You may be able to request an "extra hand" for specific activities. Consider asking for another adult for supervision during lab activities or for specific labs (such as those using fire, volatile chemicals, and live animals). This will help all of the students in the class participate fully while alleviating concerns about safety. Having more than one adult in the classroom provides an extra pair of eyes (and hands) to monitor the lab activities for the entire class (Linz, Heater, and Howard 2011).

Should you be provided with an extra adult (special education teacher, instructional assistant), please make sure to go over the lab with the individual present prior to the actual lab being conducted. The "extra help" needs to know what to look for and how to best assist you during the lab. When possible, it is recommended to run through the lab or experiment with the other person prior to having the students perform the lab (Linz, Heater, and Howard 2011). Another recommendation is to demonstrate safety procedures and equipment (fire extinguisher, eyewash station) for the adult helper so they are prepared for any contingency.

The importance of safety when conducting labs cannot be overstated; however, your own experience in teaching science will provide an excellent foundation for problem solving these issues for students with disabilities. Remember, the special education teacher can offer assistance in how to modify a lab or accommodate a specific student's disability to help ensure a safe lab experience. Chemistry teachers will find information about a helpful resource in Figure 5.2.

> **FIGURE 5.2. RESOURCE FOR CHEMISTRY TEACHERS**
>
> *The School Chemistry Laboratory Safety Guide*—jointly published by the U.S. Consumer Product Safety Commission (CPSC), the National Institute for Occupational Safety and Health (NIOSH), and the Centers for Disease Control and Prevention (CDC)—is a must-read document. It was updated in 2006 and is available online from the CDC at *www.cdc.gov/niosh/docs/2007-107.*

Lab Partners

During lab experiments, students are often assigned to work in pairs or teams to accomplish the tasks. Again, assigning lab partners and teams for performing labs is a vital component of how you teach labs; however, there are some unique challenges that may arise when including students with disabilities. You are already aware of how individual groups of students may need to learn to work together for successful lab experiences. The following discussion is intended to help you as you include students with disabilities in the advanced labs.

During a lab, you are moving around the room questioning, guiding, and coaching students on how to conduct the experiment. Often you may find that you are also refereeing student disagreements and helping students resolve differences of opinion. This should continue! Including a student with a disability should not change how you instruct students during labs.

To effectively group students for labs, you need to preplan and select students to be paired prior to the actual lab or experiment. Consider both students' knowledge of the material, ability to work with someone else, and potential personality conflicts that will be difficult for them to resolve (Potts and Howard 2011). Again, it is important to review an individual student's IEP to determine if there are specific concerns that may affect how and who you assign as lab partners. It is important that students with disabilities be grouped with their nondisabled peers (Johnson and Johnson 1986). So, if you have two students with disabilities in your classroom, do not automatically assign them as partners. You may also decide to change the composition of lab pairs throughout the school year to have students learn to work with different classmates.

Most science labs assign pairs of students to work together; however, you may want to consider groups or teams of four students for some projects, as this is effective in maximizing student learning (Howard and James 2003). This can provide the benefit of assigning each team member a specific role or responsibility to accomplish during the lab, as well as encouraging all of the students to work together. It also provides the student with a disability a smaller group of students to interact with, rather than an entire classroom. This may increase the confidence of the student with a disability and ensure more classroom success.

Students with disabilities should have the same standards for lab behavior as their peers. Just as you use a safety contract, you may want to consider using a lab partner contract or a code of conduct for partners. This document could include lab rules for partners, including items such as rules, standards for politeness, sharing of lab equipment, and a discussion of what to do when you disagree. This establishes your lab partnership standards for the entire class. Please see Figure 5.3 for some suggestions for lab partner rules.

FIGURE 5.3. LAB PARTNER RULES

Because this is an advanced class, encourage all students to think and work as though they are actual scientists. The following are rules for behavior:

- Scientists must work well with others. You should be polite and courteous to your lab partner. Please use appropriate language (no profanity) during class and labs.
- Scientists must be organized. You are reminded to maintain an organized lab space. You and your partner should take turns gathering materials, setting up the experiments, and cleaning up after experiments. Please come to labs prepared (bring pencils, notebooks).
- Scientists must collect data and report on their data. You and your lab partner must share data collection and lab report writing duties. You should plan to review your recorded data for accuracy. You may proofread each other's lab reports.
- Sometimes scientists have disagreements, but they must resolve them in a professional manner. You are reminded to resolve conflicts with your partner in a positive manner. You may ask the teacher for assistance if you cannot resolve the problem on your own.

However, some students with disabilities have disruptive behavior related to their disability and need special consideration. For example, a student who is gifted in physics may disengage during lab experiments to pace around the classroom. The student is capable of completing the work, but becomes uncomfortable when forced to work with the lab partner. You may decide to allow some pacing as a "cooling off" period but then require that the student re-engage with the experiment. Or you may allow the student to leave the classroom to chat with the guidance counselor. You can also consider if it is appropriate for the student to work on the lab alone. Once you get to know the student, you may have more potential solutions for the behavior.

It takes time to know your students; therefore, there may be some missteps or poor partnerships established at the beginning of the year. These situations need to be corrected and should not be allowed to fester, as this will diminish student learning. Should this occur with a lab pair that includes a student with a disability, the student's special education teacher may have suggestions or insight to help you problem solve. Remember, the IEP team and special education teacher can assist you in finding individual solutions for these students. The following discussion will provide some specific suggestions for lab partnerships.

Suggestions for Students With Physical Disabilities

Students with physical disabilities may have difficulty with fine motor skills (holding test tubes, using scissors) or limited mobility (use a wheelchair), which can inhibit their lab performance.

- *Assign an appropriate lab partner:* When assigning lab partners, consider students who have shown empathy and a willingness to assist their peers. The lab partner can help hold a test tube, use a Bunsen burner, and provide other assistance depending on the lab requirements. However, some students may be "overhelpful" when working with students with disabilities. Should you see this happening, please gently remind the over-helpful student that everyone needs an opportunity to try the experiment.
- *Modify physical requirements of the lab:* Encourage the student with a disability to be independent by modifying equipment or restructuring the experiment. Please see the Science Education for Students With Disabilities website for more information (*www.sesd.info/index.htm*).

Suggestions for Students With Specific Learning Disabilities

Students with specific learning disabilities may be poorly organized and/or lack focus in following directions. This behavior can be very frustrating for their lab partner and when pairing students carefully consider both students' personality and flexibility. A student who is highly organized and meticulous may not be a good partner for students with these types of disabilities, unless they have proven to be able to share that organization with peers successfully in the past.

Suggestions for Students With Social Deficits (Asperger's Syndrome, Emotional Disabilities)

Many students with this type of disability have social skill goals listed on their IEPs (Hallahan, Kauffman, and Pullen 2009). Some disabilities (Asperger's) have specific personality traits or characteristic behaviors that may be considered quirky. This quirky behavior may include behaviors such as speaking loudly at inappropriate times, refusing to work with a partner, showing interest in only one aspect of an assignment, or confronting the science teacher with excessive facts to make a point. All of these behaviors can create difficulties for both lab partners.

- *Prevent frustration:* Once you get to know these students, it may be possible to anticipate areas where the lab partnership will have difficulties. For example, a student with an emotional disability may express frustration by walking away from the partner. You can structure the lab so frustration is limited or allow the student to cool off, then return to working the experiment. You will also find that the more specific the lab directions are, the less opportunity students will have to get frustrated or have disagreements.
- *Provide coaching:* You already do this as you walk around the room, but you may want to pay extra attention to helping lab partners resolve any disagreements. For example, a student with social skill deficits may be rude to their lab partner. You may need to address the rude behavior and encourage or reassure the student who was the recipient of the behavior. When addressing an inappropriate behavior, be specific about what the student did or said, and specific about what the appropriate behavior is.
- *Create a backup plan:* For example, if the student with a disability disengages and is asked to leave the classroom, can you assign the lab partner to another group? Can he finish the experiment on his own? Is there another student who can assist him (after finishing her own work)?

Lab Reports

Once students have collected the data or the experiment is over, the students need to do an analysis of the results and write a lab report. While the lab experiments and subsequent reports will vary depending on the discipline (physics, chemistry, biology), the presentation of the data in both visual (charts, graphs) and written forms (report) is highlighted as a way for students to achieve "depth of understanding" (NRC 2002, p. 69). Writing the lab report can be challenging for any student, and students with disabilities may have serious difficulties with this task.

FOSTERING STUDENT INDEPENDENCE: LAB SAFETY AND LAB PARTNERS

Student, please ask yourself the following questions:

- Do I know the safety procedures for this lab?
- Do I have my materials (goggles, directions) prepared?
- Do I need to ask any questions of the teacher?
- Do I know my lab partner?
- Did we discuss how we will do the lab?
- What will I do first?
- What if we don't agree—what can I do?
- Who will write the down the data?
- Do I have my lab book with me?
- When is the lab report due?
- If I need help, who will I ask?

As a science teacher, you teach scientific practices and have experience in teaching how data should be collected, analyzed, and conveyed. The following discussion will focus on three areas that may present difficulties for students with disabilities that can make a lab report challenging:

- Accuracy of the data collected
- Visual representation of the data (charts and graphs)
- Written lab report

Accuracy of the Data Collected

There are many factors in the accuracy of the data collection: Did the student read the thermometer correctly? Did he measure from the proper starting point? Did she begin or end the stopwatch at the correct measuring point? While these are concerns regarding accuracy of the measurement, there are other concerns that need to be addressed, such as poor handwriting (dysgraphia) and number reversals.

Poor handwriting or the inability to hold a pen or pencil creates problems in accurate data collection. The notes from an experiment may be unreadable or the numbers for measures may be easily confused ("Is it a 2 or a 7?"). Additionally, a student may become frustrated when he is unable to read his partner's notes or data. Poor handwriting can be addressed by using technology (AlphaSmart, laptops, graphing calculators, iPads), having the other lab partner be responsible for writing down the data, or allowing partners to share their data sheets after the experiment is concluded. Please see Chapter 6 for more information on using assistive technology.

Number reversals happen frequently because they are such an easy error to make. Consider a measurement of 25 cm with a reversed number of 52 cm. These types of errors can profoundly change the outcome of an experiment. While an occasional number reversal can happen to anyone, some students with disabilities are more prone to these types of mistakes. So, you should have all students review each measurement as it is taken. In a lab partnership, one partner could write the number down and the other partner can check it for accuracy. Have students review the entire data set and ask, "Do these numbers make sense?" This process can help them identify numbers that do not make sense in the range of data collected.

Visual Representation of the Data (Chart and Graphs)

Since AP courses are intended to help students test out of undergraduate science courses, there has been a focus on both creating and interpreting charts, tables, and graphs (NRC 2002). This focus is shared by the IB and accelerated honors classes. Some disciplines may also require the creation or interpretation of diagrams or models.

The challenge of creating charts, tables, and graphs has been greatly decreased with technology. Programs like Microsoft Excel or the use of a graphing calculator have minimized the need to physically create charts with a pencil. However, some students with disabilities (visual or specific learning disabilities) do have difficulty connecting number sets to visual images. They may not be able to accurately interpret the meaning of a bar graph or pie chart. They will need practice and scaffolding to master this skill (Mastropieri and Scruggs 2010).

Consider having students create a chart or graph, then have them provide an explanation of what it represents. Consider class "warmups" that ask students to interpret a table or chart. Incorporate exercises or questions interpreting charts, tables, or graphs as part of your test preparations before students take the end-of-year examination.

Written Lab Report

Students should be taught to plan their writing and focus their attention to the task (Mastropieri and Scruggs 2010). You may already do this as part of setting up a lab experiment by foreshadowing what will happen and using a handout to guide the experiment. All students (but particularly those with difficulties in writing) can be assisted by the use of a lab report template (Linz, Heater, and Howard 2011). This template can include written prompts for the hypothesis, space for the data collection, space for the analysis, and some guiding questions to help focus the student's thoughts to be written. Templates could be handed out at the beginning of a lab to help students begin planning their report. This type of template is an example of using a graphic organizer, as discussed in Chapter 4.

This template can be a support for students until they become more proficient in writing the report. Then this support (scaffolding) can be removed and students can write the report more independently. This could be used with the entire class and removed. Or you could offer it as discreet assistance to specific students. Please see Figure 5.4 on page 84 for a Lab Report Worksheet. This example is for a physics lab; however, it can be used for any science experiments, with minor modifications to headings.

Students with disabilities may need individual support through the special education department, peer tutoring, or after-school programs to assist them in developing their writing skills. Students with disabilities can become proficient at writing lab reports with practice and guidance from the science teacher. The following discussion will provide some specific suggestions.

Suggestions for Students With Physical Disabilities

Many of these students can benefit from using technology to compensate for their physical limitations. Their lab partners may also be a source of assistance.

- Address the issue of handwriting and data collection through technology.
- Encourage the use of the Lab Report Worksheet.
- Consider physical limitations if asking students to create models or draw diagrams. (Can they accomplish the assignment through technology?)
- Please see Figure 5.5 (p. 85), "Suggestions for Students With Visual Impairments in Labs."
- Please see Figure 5.6 (p. 86), "Suggestions for Students With Hearing Impairments in Labs."

Suggestions for Students With Specific Learning Disabilities

Students with learning disabilities may need to have material organized in a way that provides for small increments of information (McCann 1998). Again, this is not related to their knowledge or understanding of the content (or analysis of the data), but may be related to the disability. For example, a student may know what happened during a chemistry experiment and accurately convey the analysis verbally, but have difficulty organizing her thoughts in writing.

- Encourage the use of the Lab Report Worksheet.
- Provide extra practice interpreting charts, graphs, and tables.
- Allow lab partners to proofread each other's work.

FIGURE 5.4. PHYSICS LAB REPORT WORKSHEET

Directions: Please note that you and your lab partner should address the following items. Once you have completed the experiment and this worksheet, then you will word-process a lab report to be graded. You and your lab partner may discuss the experiment and any calculations, then proofread and edit the final lab report before submitting it for a grade.

1. **Purpose and hypothesis**: In this section, describe what the experiment is about and what you think might happen.

2. **Procedures and equipment:** In this section, describe what you did in the experiment. Please detail what equipment you used. You can also include a drawing of how the equipment was set up.

3. **Data**: In this section, write down your "raw" data. Or, if the teacher has handed out data collection sheets, make a note of what data are being collected (time, distance). You do want to make sure you have the correct units of measure and accurate recordings of the numbers. Remember, there may be a table to complete on the data collection sheets. If so, make sure it is correctly labeled.

4. **Calculations**: In this section, write out any equations you will use. Also, write out the numbers you are using for your equations. Show the equation and all of your work for the calculations. You may use your calculator.

5. **Results**: In this section, show any tables or graphs that you are asked to complete. This should be a summary of the data. You should also provide a couple of sentences of explanation of the data .

6. **Conclusion**: In this section, summarize the experiment in your own words, describe what was learned, and note any errors or mistakes that might have happened. You might describe how the experiment could be improved next time.

Remember, once this worksheet is completed, you will word process a lab report to be submitted for grading. This worksheet and any data collection sheets must be attached to your word-processed final lab report to earn full credit.

Suggestions for Students With Social Deficits (Asperger's Syndrome, Emotional Disabilities)

Some students will resist assignments that require writing. They may not turn in lab reports or finish the assignment before submitting it for grading. This may be identified on their IEP. These students should not be exempt from all writing assignments unless it is specifically stated on their IEP. Please refer to the accommodations and modifications discussion in Chapter 2.

- Encourage the use of the Lab Report Worksheet.
- Allow lab partners to proofread each other's work.
- Consult with a special education teacher if you need strategies to encourage completion of writing assignments.

FIGURE 5.5. SUGGESTIONS FOR INCLUDING STUDENTS WITH VISUAL IMPAIRMENTS IN LABS

- Provide handouts or directions (any print materials) with a large-size font for students who have low or limited vision. You might want to do this for classroom signs, too.
- Use talking calculators, thermometers, probes, and other equipment that provide auditory signals.
- Provide tactile drawings (with raised edges) or three-dimensional models that students can feel. Glue guns can be used to provide raised drawings. Simply use the glue gun to heat the glue and trace an image. Once the glue has cooled, there is a raised "image" that the student can feel. For example, you could trace different types of leaves with the hot glue, leaving a raised edge so that a visually impaired student could feel the difference between a pine needle and a maple leaf.
- Provide lab equipment such as beakers with raised measurement graduations or notches. Check with the company that supplies your lab equipment; they may have some of these items.
- Provide clearly stated verbal directions.
- Consider providing tactile markers on lab equipment to help the student identify it (think sandpaper on a draw pull, different shape buttons on a cabinet or shelves)
- Consider using handouts and worksheets that are in Braille.
- Provide enhanced or larger images by connecting TV monitors to microscopes or large panel monitors to computers.
- Review the National Center for Blind Youth in Science website (*www.blindscience.org/ncbys/For_Teachers_and_Parents.asp?SnID=503018803*). This website has a resource center where you can obtain tactile models, lab equipment, and teacher resources.

FIGURE 5.6. SUGGESTIONS FOR INCLUDING STUDENTS WITH HEARING IMPAIRMENTS IN LABS

- Provide preferential seating for the student. This may be upfront in the classroom near where you provide instruction; however, in a lab, it might be a station that you can easily move to as you provide assistance.
- Provide closed-captioning on all classroom videos and computer simulations. Make sure to enable the function prior to showing the simulation or video.
- When providing directions or instruction, face the student. Do not talk to their back or shout.
- Some students will benefit when you use a microphone. Please check with the special education teacher.
- Provide all directions verbally and in writing. You might provide individual written instructions as handouts or write them on the blackboard.
- Provide visual warning lights or signals.

Field Trips

Field trips are an exciting way to expand classroom learning. A well-planned field trip can be a terrific opportunity to gather data in the real world or learn more about a specific concept through a museum presentation, planetarium visit, or community resource. When planning for a field trip, it is important to include all of the students (Potts and Howard 2011).

FOSTERING STUDENT INDEPENDENCE: FIELD TRIPS

Student, please ask yourself the following:

- Do I have the permission slip?
- When is the field trip? Do I have anything else due on that day?
- Where are we going?
- Do I need to bring anything (lunch, money, notebook)?
- Do I have a field trip buddy? If so, who is it?
- What if I get separated from the class? Where do I go for help?
- Is there a follow-up assignment? Do I have to do anything on the field trip?
- If the field trip ends late, how will I get home?
- Do I have my parents' contact information with me?

FIGURE 5.7. FIELD TRIP CHECKLIST

1. Does the date work with the school calendar?
2. Have you obtained approval from the appropriate authorities for the trip?
3. Is the destination appropriate for learning?
4. How many students can the trip accommodate?
5. What kind of transportation will be used?
6. What forms and documents do you need the students and parents to complete?
    - o Emergency care cards with contact numbers
    - o Parent or guardian permission forms
    - o Insurance verification for drivers
    - o Releases from other teachers
    - o Any other local forms
7. How many chaperones do you need?
8. Is there funding, or will the students pay?
9. Will students need spending money?
10. Will you need to find a place for lunch, or can the students bring a bag lunch?
11. What first-aid supplies and student medications will you need to take?
12. What is the appropriate attire?
13. Do you have a written agenda?
    - o Exactly what will happen during the field trip?
    - o Do you need to plan places to convene at different times during the day?
    - o Where will you meet the students at the end of the day?
14. Do you need extra supplies?
    - o Sunscreen
    - o Bug repellant
15. Do you have contingency plans?
    - o Weather (Do students need to bring appropriate outerwear?)
    - o Do you cancel the field trip in event of weather (such as rain or snow)?
16. Do you have a procedure to collect appropriate receipts and documentation?
17. Have you made arrangements to ensure that all students will be met by parents at the end of the field trip, if the return is after school hours?

Source: Linz, Heater, and Howard 2011. Used with permission.

CHAPTER 5

In your prior field trips, you may not have had to consider a student with disruptive behavior, a student who becomes disoriented in new locations, or a student who needs a ramp to enter a building. You will need to carefully consider where the field trip is going to be, how the students will engage at the site, and how the individual student with a disability can participate. Some behavior that may be acceptable in a site at or near the school (school garden, basketball gym) may not be acceptable at a science museum or planetarium.

Depending on the proposed site for the field trip, you may believe that some students' behavior may preclude their participation in outings off school grounds. Prior to any decision to exclude a student from a field trip, you should carefully consider other options (Potts and Howard 2011). You must have a thorough discussion with the IEP team regarding your concerns. It is recommended that you and the IEP team discuss potential ways in which the student can participate. Remember that the students' parents and the student are members of the IEP team. They should also be involved in the conversation.

These students have been placed in your advanced class because they are capable of doing the work; therefore, do not automatically assume that they cannot successfully participate in a field trip. They can! Some students can be successful if provided foreshadowing of what they will encounter on the field trip. You may even consider assigning all students a partner or field trip buddy (Linz, Heater, and Howard 2011).

The key to a successful experience is *prior planning* to alleviate any potential concerns. You can contact the site to ensure that it will be accessible to all of your students and discuss any special requirements that your students may have. Many locations (museums, zoos) have a liaison person for science teachers who can ensure that all of your students will have a good experience during the field trip. The liaison can be helpful in coordinating your visit.

This is also a time when you may want to request an additional adult to accompany the group on the field trip. You can always ask for parent volunteers to help supervise the field trip. Parents of students with disabilities may be very interested in going along on the trip, especially for students with other health impairments such as diabetes or epilepsy. Or maybe the special education teacher would like to go with you. Sometimes a paraprofessional or instructional assistant can be assigned to go on the field trip. It is not appropriate to disallow a child from attending a field trip based only on their disability categorization, though it may take more planning on your part, especially if students will require medications while on the trip.

Again, field trips are an important part of learning in the advanced classroom, so you should continue to include them in your curriculum. Find ways in which all of the students (including those with challenging behaviors) can successfully participate. Please see Figure 5.7 (p. 87) for a field trip checklist for science teachers.

Independent Research

The National Research Council (2002) recommends that students be provided the opportunity to formulate their own research questions and design ways in which to explore their questions (inquiry-based). Many advanced classes have incorporated student projects that focus on student-designed and student-conducted research. These types of student projects vary depending on the science discipline. You may already use a student research project in your teaching. This should continue!

Students with disabilities can and should conduct their own research projects under your guidance. The preceding discussion has provided you with an overview of potential difficulties and some solutions; however, independent research may have some challenging aspects for some students with disabilities. Consider the following:

- A student with physical limitations may need extra support to set up and run an experiment.
- A student with specific learning disabilities may need support to organize the research project into manageable components that build on each other in a logical way.
- A student with social deficits may need support in enlisting other people's support for their project.

As you get to know your students, you should know what supports will be necessary for their success.

Another element of independent research is the participation of students in science contests, such as those by Siemens or Intel. Many science teachers encourage their classes to enter these contests or science fairs. Some contests allow team entries. Students with disabilities should be encouraged to participate both individually and in a team. Should a student with disabilities choose to enter such a contest, please share information with the student's special education teacher so he can provide help to the student in organizing the entry. The following websites are just a sample of these contests:

Intel

- Intel International Science and Engineering Fair: *www.intel.com/about/corporateresponsibility/education/isef/index.htm*

- Intel Science Talent Search: *www.intel.com/about/corporateresponsibility/education/sts/index.htm*

Siemens

- Siemens Foundation Competition: *www.siemens-foundation.org/en/competition.htm*

Independent research is an important component of learning how to be a scientist, and students with disabilities can be successful. Please note that there is an increased awareness and desire to encourage students with disabilities to participate in scientific research at the college level, and independent research

FIGURE 5.8. RESOURCE

The National Science Foundation (NSF) has a particular interest in expanding the participation of students with disabilities in STEM (science, technology, engineering, and math) programs. Please note that some of the projects do have funding for undergraduate students pursuing an interest in STEM programs. Consider sharing this information with the school guidance office as they help students plan the transition to college. For more information, please see the NSF website (*www.nsf.gov/funding/pgm_summ.jsp?pims_id=5482*).

FOSTERING STUDENT INDEPENDENCE: INDIVIDUAL RESEARCH

Student, please ask yourself the following questions:

- What is my research question? (What do I want to know?)
- How can I find out the answer?
- What materials do I need?
- How should I set up the experiment?
- What data do I need?
- How will I collect the data?
- How will I analyze the data?
- Do I need a chart, graph, or table to show the data?
- How will I share my findings and conclusions?

Note: You may already have a handout that encompasses these questions as part of your student project.

helps students develop research skills. Please see Figure 5.8 for information on a National Science Foundation (NSF) initiative.

Conclusion

You are knowledgeable about the importance of labs and data collection and analysis in the advanced classroom. Hopefully you have been reassured that your experiences are important to how you accommodate students with disabilities in your classroom. You should have noted that many of the suggestions in this chapter are simple to incorporate without fundamentally changing your teaching. Many of the suggestions can easily be used with the entire class, thus providing all students with supports for success.

IDEAS TO GET YOU STARTED

- Review the student's IEP.
- Use a safety contract.
- Ask for an adult helper (for some labs).
- Plan for assignment of work stations.
- Select and coach lab partners.
- Create a backup plan for when things go wrong.
- Review the field trip checklist.
- Assist students in developing their own research.

References

Centers for Disease Control and Prevention. 2006. *School chemistry laboratory safety guide. www.cdc.gov/niosh/docs/2007-107*

College Entrance Examination Board. 2001. *Advanced placement course description: Physics.* New York: College Entrance Examination Board.

Hallahan, D. P., J. M. Kauffman, and P. C. Pullen. 2009. *Exceptional learners: An introduction to special education.* 11th ed. New York: Allyn & Bacon, Pearson Education.

Howard, L., and A. James. 2003. *What principals need to know about... differentiated instruction.* Arlington, VA: Educational Research Service (ERS) and National Association of Elementary School Principals (NAESP).

Johnson, D. W., and R. T. Johnson. 1986. Mainstreaming and cooperative learning strategies. *Exceptional Children* 52 (6): 553–561.

Linz, E., M. J. Heater, and L. A. Howard. 2011. *Team teaching science: Success for all learners.* Arlington, VA: National Science Teachers Association.

Mastropieri, M. A., and T. E. Scruggs. 2010. *The inclusive classroom: Strategies for effective instruction*. 4th ed. Upper Saddle River, NJ: Pearson.

McCann, W. S. 1998. Science classrooms for students with special needs. *ERIC Digest.* ED433185. Columbus, OH: ERIC Clearinghouse for Science Mathematics and Environmental Education.

National Center for Blind Youth in Science. 2011. *www.blindscience.org.*

National Research Council (NRC). 2002. *Learning and understanding: Improving advanced study of mathematics and science in U.S. high schools.* Committee on Programs for Advanced Study of Mathematics and Science in American High Schools. J. P. Gollub, M. W. Bertenthal, J. B. Labov, and P. C. Curtis, eds. Center for Education. Division of Behavioral and Social Science and Education. Washington, DC: National Academies Press.

Potts, E. A., and L. A. Howard. 2011. *How to co-teach: A guide for general and special educators.* Baltimore, MD: Brookes Publishing.

Roy, K. 2010. Safer science. *The Science Teacher* 77 (3): 10–11.

Science Education for Students with Disabilities. *www.sesd.info/index.htm*

CHAPTER 6

Assistive Technology and Your Classroom

In recent years, there has been an explosion of technological advances for classrooms. Students use laptops to write their lab reports, graphing calculators to record measurements during experiments, and sometimes their smartphones to manage their assignment due dates. You use technology in your teaching. Many districts have instructional technology specialists working in schools to make sure all of your computer and technology needs are met. So, you are very familiar with how technology is used in classrooms, but may not be as familiar with specialized uses of technology to support students with disabilities.

Incorporation of technology into the advanced classroom has flourished as the national focus on success in STEM classes has accelerated (NRC 2002). The assumption is that new technologies support student learning of scientific concepts and processes. You may have attended special trainings or obtained new equipment or software in your classroom for the teaching of science as part of this increased focus on technology.

This has also happened with specialized technology to support students with disabilities. In fact, the availability and emphasis on technology is likely to continue and may include products that are not yet developed. However, being receptive to new and current technologies will help many of your students with disabilities maximize learning opportunities. The following discussion provides an overview of important terminology, some examples of how you can use current technologies, and suggestions for working with the IEP team and instructional technologist. We assume that you are already familiar with using technology for teaching science. This discussion will provide you with an overview of the types and uses of technology to support students with disabilities in your classroom.

CHAPTER 6

Overview of Assistive Technology

You may already know "instructional technology" or "educational technology" as the broad terms for the use of computers, electronic tools, and software in your classroom. Many of the devices, computers, and software programs used in your classroom adhere to principles of Universal Design for Learning (UDL), which means that the technologies have been designed with features that enable both students with disabilities and their nondisabled peers to use the devices or programs. So, you may be able to assist some of your students with disabilities using your current classroom computer, devices, and software programs—for example, you could view a web video with closed captioning for a student with a hearing impairment. For more information on the concept of universal design, please refer back to Chapter 1.

Assistive technology (AT) refers to the use of technology to *assist* or improve the performance of a student with a disability (Puckett 2005). An important consideration is that the definition of *technology* is not limited to computer technology. You may be familiar with grab bars, walkers, or eyeglasses. These are all examples of assistive technologies that are not computer- or electronic-based. Technology can be any device, item, or product that can help a student with a disability increase his capabilities (U.S. Department of Education 2012), though the following discussion will focus on electronic devices, computer systems, and applications.

Additionally, assistive technology can also be classified as low tech or high tech. Low-tech technology traditionally includes technologies that are cheap, readily available, and often easy to create, while high-tech AT often needs electricity, requires specialized programs, is more expensive, and is harder to use unobtrusively. An example of low-tech assistive technology might be a ruler with large numbers that can be easily read by students with visual impairments, while high-tech assistive technology might include an electronic dictionary that students can speak into and have the word definition appear on screen.

Assistive technology can be further refined into categories of Type I or Type II. Type I is often called a closed system, which means that the user has limited choices and controls. Think of a software program for addressing curricular goals that has the student review material or answer questions but does not allow the user (student) to deviate from a programmed path (Puckett 2005). Think of software that students can use as a worksheet for review. Type II is often called an open system, which means that the user has more options and controls. Think of a voice-activated program or text-to-speech synthesizer where the user (student) can create new options and content (Puckett 2005).

While you may read or hear these terms when you have a student with a disability in your class, what is more important for you is how the student will use the technology or if a student with disabilities will use AT in your classroom. Not all students with disabilities need AT. For some students, your regular classroom technology can function as AT. For example, you can enlarge a font size on a computer monitor so that it can be easily read by students with limited vision. Not all AT needs to be specialized; AT just needs to help improve the student's classroom performance.

AT Devices (Tools)

The potential of smartphones, tablets (such as the iPad), and e-readers is just beginning to be explored; however, it is apparent that these devices can provide an affordable AT solution for many students with disabilities. Actually, many of your students, not just those with disabilities, use smartphones, e-readers, and tablets, so you may have experience with their functions. For example, the calendar and agenda functions in a smartphone can easily be used as an electronic planner by students. They can record assignment due dates and manage their schedules. Some textbooks can be downloaded to an e-reader so a student does not need to carry a textbook in her book bag. Currently, the number of textbooks available on e-readers is limited, but the number is expected to grow in the next few years.

Another device, the AlphaSmart, provides a keyboard and the ability to take notes or type. These devices are sturdy and inexpensive, as they do not have all of the features of a laptop but provide a keyboard and basic word processing functions (spell check, thesaurus) for students to use. Students with disabilities who have difficulty holding a pen or pencil can benefit from using these devices to take notes or write lab reports. These devices also minimize distractions because students do not have the option of changing the font size or color or adding graphics. These are also a good device for any student who needs access to a keyboard and writing instrument, including those who cannot afford a personal laptop. Many schools purchase these for use in classrooms.

Tablets (such as iPads) can be another device used as AT. These (and smartphones) are often called "mobile touch-screen devices" because they are handheld devices that activate with a tap or touch to the screen (Wilson 2011). Although research data on student use is limited, students like using these devices (Wilson 2011). These devices can include a variety of reference-type information such as a dictionary, thesaurus, calculator, and teacher notes. These added reference items can be useful for students with disabilities who may need to look up an unknown word. They are relatively inexpensive when compared to other AT and are very popular for home use, meaning that many students already have them. Some schools are even purchasing them for students.

Apple devices (such as the iPhone, iPad, and iPod) incorporate special design features that increase accessibility for people with disabilities. VoiceOver comes on Apple computers and can be available for other Apple devices (iPhone, iPad). This application allows a user to touch an element on the screen and hear a description of what it is. While Apple provides this application, not all makers of applications for Apple products use this feature. So, if you need this feature to work for a student when using a particular application, please have someone check to make sure it is enabled (Wilson 2011). Zoom is another built-in feature that magnifies what is on the screen. Both Zoom and VoiceOver can be useful for students with visual impairments and students with learning disabilities who need auditory cues (Wilson 2011). Apple also includes a closed-captioning feature in their devices (Wilson 2011), which allows a user to read subtitles. This feature can be used by students with hearing impairments and students with auditory processing deficits.

Another important aspect of tablets and smartphones are the applications (or "apps") that can operate on the device. Both tablets and smartphones have a plethora of apps available that can provide support for both learning science content and organizing and managing student assignments. Apps for Apple devices can be downloaded at the Apple App store. Some apps are free, while others cost a small amount. Wilson (2011) describes the following small sample of apps that may be helpful to your students:

- *The Elements: A Visual Exploration (published by the Element Collection, Inc.):* This application is an interactive periodic table of the elements.
- *Speak it! (published by Future Apps, Inc.):* This is a text-to-speech application that students can use for editing and proofreading their documents. The application highlights each word of text as it reads the word aloud.
- *WritePad (published by PhatWare Corp.):* This is a handwriting-to-text application. Students who write by hand (e.g., notes) can have the application translate their handwriting into typed text.
- *Audio-Note and NotePad (published by Luminant Software):* This is a note-taking application where students write the key word and the teacher's lecture is recorded. The application then synchronizes the writing and voice in a playback mode.
- *iHomework (published by Paul Pilone):* This is a student-specific application for managing homework assignments, grades, and schedules, as well as tracking progress on long-term assignments.
- *iThoughts (published by CMS):* This is a concept-mapping application that can provide visual assistance to students.

Please note that the apps listed are not just for students with disabilities; any student might find them helpful. New apps are always being developed, and you should plan to occasionally review (or check reviews of) them. You may find something that provides a unique aspect that you can use in your classroom or that a student may find helpful.

Another device becoming more common is the digital pen (also known as SmartPen). This pen has a small recording device inside that records the lecture while the student is writing notes. These devices are relatively inexpensive (around $100), and having the recording with key words can help students take better notes. There is a similar application where a note-taking device is linked through a USB port to a computer; the audio recording is then transferred into text, creating a typed document of notes. IRISNotes and SmartPen by Livescribe are two of the commercially available products that students might find helpful. Please note that the iPad also has a note-taking app that was described earlier in this chapter. Of course, an old-fashioned tape recorder can also be used to record a lecture. Students will still have to take their own notes, but they can listen to the actual recording numerous times to help their recall. Not all useful technology is recently developed!

Another important consideration is that these devices (tablets, smartphones) are also used in college. Since students in your class are on a pathway to college, using these devices will provide important experience. For example, students will learn what organizing and time-management app works best for them, or if a note-taking app helps their recall of information. Please see Table 6.1 (p. 98) for a few examples of technology supports for learning difficulties.

Software and the Internet

Just as there are many different devices, there are many types of software programs. Keep in mind that many of the software programs you and your students already use may have special features that enable all students, including those with disabilities, to use them. If you have not already done so, you may want to spend some time exploring any software that you use in your classroom, or at least ask the instructional technologist if he or she knows of any specialized features that might help a student in your classroom.

Simulation software, through which experiments can be done with changing variables over many trials, has become common in the advanced classroom. You may be familiar with the virtual cat or frog dissection software and websites. In fact, the College Board offers many suggestions for using this type of software in Advanced Placement (AP) science classes (College Board 2012). The College Board also provides teacher resources for both software and web-based simulation at their AP Central website in the section "Teacher Resources." Students with disabilities can benefit from the opportunity to run an experiment many times

TABLE 6.1. EXAMPLES OF TECHNOLOGY SUPPORTS FOR LEARNING DIFFICULTIES

Type of Technology (Devices and Software)	Difficulties That Technology Addresses
Closed captioning: Available on TVs, computer video, Apple products (iPhones, iPads, Macs)	Provides words that can be read on the screen. Useful for students with hearing impairments and those who have difficulty processing auditory information.
Text readers: Available on e-readers and computer video and as software that can be purchased	Provides a read-aloud version of printed words. Useful for students with visual impairments and those who have difficulty reading. A similar application can highlight text as it is read. This is useful for proofreading and editing documents.
Speech to text: Available as software (Dragon) and on devices such as SmartPens and Apple products (iPhones, iPads)	Provides typing (word processing) of spoken words. The words are typed as they are spoken. Useful for students with physical impairments that limit their physical writing ability.
Handwriting to text: Available as software and an iPad application	Provides text once a student has handwritten notes. Useful for students who may need text for ease of reading.
Electronic planners: Calendars and reminders that are available on a wide variety of devices (Smartphones, computers, tablets)	Provides students both visual and auditory cues for managing their time and assignment due dates.
Note-taking devices: Available as SmartPens, digital pens, other devices with recording features (iPhone, iPad)	Provides students with the ability to record spoken words and take written notes simultaneously
Concept-mapping: Available as software (Inspiration) and as an application for the iPad	Provides students with the ability to create and review concept maps (visual representations) of ideas

without having to physically set up the equipment. The software also provides a visual of how the changing variables can affect the outcome of the experiment.

The use of web-based videos and simulations can also assist students with disabilities for the same reasons. They can explore the web content during class and on their own time. The visual and auditory information can easily be repeated to help the student's understanding (Richardson and Beard 2008). Please see Figure 6.1 for a list of websites for labs.

FIGURE 6.1. WEBSITES FOR INTERACTIVE LABS

- Biology Labs
    - Mitochondria Lab: *http://biologylab.awlonline.com*
    - University of Alberta, Department of Biological Science, Instructional Multimedia: *www.biology.ualberta.ca/facilities/multimedia*
- Chemistry Labs
    - The Chemistry Place: *http://chemplace.com*
    - The Laboratory Notebook: *www.chemtopics.com/aplab/contents.htm*
- Physics Labs
    - Teaching Advanced Physics (TAP) from the Institute of Physics (IOP) Resources for Teachers: *www.iop.org/education/teacher/resources/teaching-advanced-physics/page_44149.html*
    - Mississippi State WebTop online resources for teaching about lasers and optics: *http://webtop.msstate.edu/index.html*

There are also websites and software programs that are not science related that your students may find beneficial. For example, Inspiration (Inspiration Software, Inc.) is a program that provides for concept mapping that some students find useful for providing visual linkages for complex interactions. Inspiration is available as computer software or an iPad application. You may want to solicit the input of both the special education teacher and instructional technologist for their suggestions on what might be most useful to your students.

Students are also adept at using the new technology of social media and e-mail to communicate with others. This can include communication with actual scientists at major universities, students in different countries, and researchers. Although this can be a dynamic addition to classroom discussions, there may also be inappropriate uses of social media. Please see Figure 6.2 for more information.

FIGURE 6.2. A NOTE ABOUT SOCIAL MEDIA

In recent years, students have rapidly increased their use of social media, via Facebook, Twitter, Skype, and similar websites. Concurrently, these applications have also been used as a way to bully other students. Students with disabilities are more likely than their nondisabled peers to be bullied (Sabornie and deBettencourt 2009). Many schools have established policies against bullying and for the appropriate use of social media. Please know your school's policies and be aware that students with disabilities may be bullied through social media.

Specialized AT

Some students with disabilities need very specialized AT to perform in a classroom. For example, you may have a student whose physical disability affects his ability to speak. This student may communicate via a speech synthesizer. They have a keyboard or other device that types out words that are then "read" by a computer and spoken aloud using a computer-generated "voice." You may be familiar with Stephen Hawking, the physicist who uses a wheelchair and a speech synthesizer to communicate.

Something to keep in mind is that people with disabilities who communicate through electronic devices are often thought to be less able than their peers. This bias can create even more difficulties for your students with disabilities as the process of communication through these devices can be time consuming. So, while it may take time for them to express their thoughts and ideas, they are just as capable as their nondisabled peers. Obviously, in the case of Stephen Hawking, no one would question his scientific ability despite the slowness of his communication.

Students who are blind or have vision impairments may also have unique AT needs. Much of how we teach science is visual. This can limit how you teach science to the student with vision impairments. We must rely on auditory, tactile, and olfactory cues to help students grasp the concepts. The use of computers that can read text aloud or describe verbally what is happening on a video becomes very important. Your school may have (or have access to) a specialist for students who are blind or have vision impairments; please contact this specialist, as he or she may have suggestions on both AT and materials that can be used in your science class. Please see Figure 6.3 for a few resources that may assist you when working with a student with a vision impairment in your advanced classroom.

FIGURE 6.3. RESOURCES FOR SCIENCE AND STUDENTS WHO ARE BLIND OR VISUALLY IMPAIRED

- Perkins School for the Blind, Resources for Science Education: *www.perkins.org/resources/scout/education/science-education*
- National Center for Blind Youth in Science: *www.blindscience.org*
- Institute for Broadening Participation, Innovations in STEM Education for Blind Undergraduates Using Digital Pen-Based Audio/Tactile Graphics: *www.pathwaystoscience.org/programhub.asp?sort=RDE-SmithKettlewell-DigitalPen*

All of these resources have links to AT for the blind or visually impaired and lists of where to purchase specific materials (e.g., tactile or auditory materials) used in science classes.

Students who are deaf or hearing impaired also have specialized AT needs. For example, they may wear hearing aids or have cochlear implants. Yes, hearing aids and cochlear implants are also AT. Teachers should be aware that hearing aids need batteries, and students should have an extra supply with them. Occasionally batteries will run low, making it difficult for a student to hear. You might want to ask the speech-language clinician or instructional technologist if there is a school supply of extra batteries for these situations when the student does not have a battery replacement. On rare occasions, students may actually turn off their hearing aids or cochlear implant because too much auditory input can be tiring or overwhelming. Most students in an advanced class will not want to miss important auditory information, but please be aware of fatigue in students who are deaf or have hearing impairments.

For some students, you may be asked to use an FM radio system. You will wear a small microphone and your voice will be amplified so the student can hear you better. These systems are easy to use, but make sure the microphone is turned off when you do not want the student to hear a private conversation (such as when you are chatting between classes with another teacher). Please feel free to ask the educational audiologist, speech-language clinician, or instructional technologist if you have any questions.

There are various types of specialized AT, including Braille to speech, speech to text, text to speech, and other applications. Most important is your willingness to work with students who have these specialized needs. While it may be a little intimidating at first, with practice you can become familiar with the different functions of these applications. Your students will appreciate your willingness to try to learn a new technology. In many situations, students are more fluent with the new technologies and can help us make adjustments. In some cases, it may be helpful to ask the student with a disability using AT to show you how to troubleshoot a device or application.

Working With the Instructional Technologist

As part of the IEP, students with disabilities are evaluated to determine if AT would help improve their performance and what types of AT would be most useful for them. This is often done by the instructional technologist and can be a time-consuming process. The evaluation process may take up the majority of a school year as the student's classroom needs are assessed, the student tries the technology, and adjustments made to the technology. Once a student is determined to need AT, the school should provide the technology at no cost to the parents (Lee and Templeton 2008). Technology can be expensive, and this provision of IDEA can be costly for schools. Nonetheless, the school must provide technology if it will benefit the student's educational performance and is written into the IEP.

For students in your advanced classroom, the evaluation process can be frustrating. They need the technology to succeed, but it may not always work or may need adjustment. Your input is important to provide more information on what works, what needs to be changed, how the technology is working for the individual student, and what you need to do to help the student work with the technology. Just as this can be frustrating for the student, it can also be very frustrating for you. Your lessons can be disrupted as the student struggles to get the device to work. Please feel free to ask the instructional technologist or special education teacher to observe in your classroom to provide support for the student and suggestions for you.

You may also want to document or make notes about what AT problems you have noted in your class (Lee and Templeton 2008). This could include battery or power concerns, physical use of a device, down times when the device or application is not working, and how the student uses the device or application in your class. Please plan to share these notes with the IEP team, including the instructional technologist. For example, if a device uses so much power that the device must be recharged for large portions of time in your class, it is not very useful to the student. If the student has physical limitations and the device is not easy to use, then it may not be an appropriate piece of technology for that student.

As you become knowledgeable about AT and your students, your input on the purchase of device and apps will be important to the IEP team. Please plan to provide input and suggestions for devices and apps that might benefit your students. Please see Figure 6.4 for some considerations and suggestions on acquiring apps, devices, and software.

FIGURE 6.4. AT: TEACHER CONSIDERATIONS

- What features does the application, software, or device have that can assist students?
- Did I check an educational review site such as *www.iear.org*?
- Is it easy for the student to use in my classroom? Is it easy for me to use?
- Can an existing device, software, or application provide the same functionality?
- Does the device, application, or software adhere to principles of Universal Design for Learning (UDL)?

The instructional technologist is the expert on the technology and how students work best with the technology; however, you are still the expert on your class and science content. Please feel free to communicate when something goes wrong or when something works really well. The instructional technologist can make better decisions on technology purchases and student use with your input.

FOSTERING STUDENT INDEPENDENCE

Students, please consider the following questions about the device or app:

- How will this device help me succeed in science class?
- Can I quickly learn to use this device or app?
- Does it help me manage my time and assignments better?
- Is it easy to use?
- Will I use it?
- Will I be able to keep track of it, or will it be easily lost?
- What do I want the technology to help me do?

Conclusion

In this chapter, we discussed how students with disabilities may use AT in your classroom. The instructional technologist can assist you as you work with students and new technologies. Please remember that students with disabilities can succeed in your advanced classroom. Although there are many devices, software programs, and apps available, your openness to trying new technologies in your classroom is more important for your students' success. The purpose of AT is to

IDEAS TO GET YOU STARTED

- Identify which students will use AT.
- Contact the instructional technologist to touch base.
- Review your current classroom technology; what features can be used as AT?
- Explore new applications and devices to see how they work and if they can be used as AT.
- Resolve to be willing to try new technologies.

help make it easier for students with disabilities to reach their potential. AT is just another way to support students with disabilities.

References

College Board. 2012. Advanced Placement teacher resources. *http://sitesearch.collegeboard.org/?q=*&tp=ap&lnd=1*

Lee, H., and R. Templeton. 2008. Ensuring equal access to technology: Providing assistive technology to students with disabilities. *Theory Into Practice* 47: 212–219.

National Research Council (NRC). 2002. Learning and understanding: Improving advanced study of mathematics and science in U.S. high schools. Committee on Programs for Advanced Study of Mathematics and Science in American High Schools. J. P. Gollub, M. W. Bertenthal, J. B. Labov, and P. C. Curtis, eds. Center for Education. Division of Behavioral and Social Science and Education. Washington, DC: National Academies Press.

Puckett, K. 2005. An assistive technology toolkit: Type II applications for students with mild disabilities. *Computers in the Schools* 22 (3/4): 107–117.

Richardson, D., and L. A. Beard. 2008. Working with students with disabilities in the general science classroom. *Special Education Technology Practice* (January/February): 27–29.

Sabornie, E. J., and L. U. deBettencourt. 2009. *Teaching students with mild and high-incidence disabilities at the secondary level.* 3rd ed. Upper Saddle River, NJ: Merrill.

Wilson, M. 2011. APPSsolutely accommodating. *Journal of Special Education Technology* 26 (2): 55–60.

U.S. Department of Education, Office of Special Education and Rehabilitative Services. 2012. Assistive Technology. *http://www2.ed.gov/programs/paat/index.html*

CHAPTER 7

End-of-Year Testing

Students who are enrolled in Advanced Placement (AP) and International Baccalaureate (IB) courses take a year-end test administered by the College Board (for AP work) or IB. Students enrolled in honors or accelerated science classes may also take end-of-the-school-year tests; however, these are not typically administered by a third party, so the student will automatically receive accommodations listed on the IEP. For students in IB or AP, the process of registering for and taking these tests depends on whether the College Board or IB administers the test. Students with disabilities who are enrolled in these courses must request the needed testing accommodations (or must have the accommodations requested on their behalf). Each agency has its own procedures, forms, and guidelines that must be followed, and accommodations may not be allowed simply because the IEP team decided they were necessary the rest of the school year. Most important, the student, parents, and IEP team must plan ahead. Requesting accommodations for a third-party assessor can be a time-consuming process.

Both the AP and IB tests are summative assessments because they gauge, or "sum up," a student's overall performance and knowledge in a subject. We understand that this passing rate is important to you as a science teacher; administrators may track the passing rate of students taking your course, using it as a measure of your effectiveness in teaching advanced science content. Your concerns regarding student performance may be amplified when including students with disabilities in your advanced classroom. Remember that these students are capable of doing the work and can perform to a high standard on the end-of-year tests, so your pass rates should stay stable.

AP and IB teachers often have students take practice tests to help prepare for these high-stakes tests. Students with disabilities should take these practice tests *with their test accommodations*. This is another reason that students with accommodations should be encouraged to use them from the beginning of the school year—so that they can practice under similar conditions to the actual test. Again, you may want to address this issue at an initial meeting with the student and the special education teacher.

Because each agency has its own process, the agencies will be discussed separately. This discussion is intended to provide an overview, and any questions regarding individual students should be directed to the appropriate entity. You may want to contact your school's guidance or college preparatory office for further information. There often is a designated contact person in your school who is responsible for requesting testing accommodations for students with disabilities. Please know your school's process and contact person.

Advanced Placement (AP)

The College Board oversees the AP curriculum and testing. For the 2010–2011 school year, more than 18,000 schools in the United States had AP courses, with more than 3 million examinations administered (College Board 2011). Because one of the purposes of AP classes is to test out of college-level courses, there is great emphasis on passing this test.

These tests are administered in May, but the exact schedule varies year to year. Please check the College Board's AP website for complete details. As you are probably aware, the College Board has a fee structure for these tests. Each individual school or school district has policies on who pays these costs. Some schools pay the fees for students, while other schools require the parents to pay. In either case, please make sure you inform parents of the school policies regarding payment of these fees.

The College Board requires parental consent and eligibility forms when requesting testing accommodations; these forms are available online. Please see Figure 7.1 for the College Board's website for students with disabilities. The school may submit these forms online. In some cases, a parent may decide to seek testing accommodations for their student directly, instead of having the school submit the request, and the College Board accepts these requests. Please note that just because the parent or school submits the forms does not mean that the College Board will provide the requested accommodations.

FIGURE 7.1. WEBSITE FOR COLLEGE BOARD STUDENT WITH DISABILITIES

This is the website for students with disabilities and it provides information on how to request testing accommodations. The website also includes downloadable forms for use when requesting accommodations. The website is located at *www.collegeboard.com/ssd/student/index.html*.

Students, their parents, and you should be aware that having testing accommodations listed on the individual student's IEP does not automatically qualify the student for testing accommodations on College Board tests. The student (or someone on her behalf) must submit a request for accommodations and provide documentation of the student's disability and need for the accommodation. The student must meet the eligibility criteria established by the College Board. In some cases, the College Board may require testing by someone (such as a psychologist) outside of the school system as part of the necessary documentation. This is a costly and time-consuming process.

We recommend that once a student with a disability is placed in your AP classroom and needs testing accommodations, you contact the IEP team to establish who will be responsible for coordinating the request to the College Board. Remember that in Chapter 2 we discussed the importance of a student's transition plan. It may be appropriate for the student to have "Request testing accommodations from the College Board" written into this transition plan during an IEP meeting. This can help ensure that the request is submitted in a timely manner and identifies a specific person who will be responsible.

The College Board also administers the SAT and PSAT exams. Once a student has been granted accommodations for any College Board exam (such as the AP test), it is easy to apply the accommodations to other examinations (such as the SAT and PSAT). In other words, the eligibility documentation does not have to be duplicated. The student's transition plan may delineate actions regarding college preparation (registering for the SAT); therefore, plan to check in with the student's guidance counselor to make sure that accommodations are in place for all College Board tests.

You may solicit the assistance of the special education teacher to make sure students are reminded about what items they will need at the testing center (identification, entry ticket). Please remind students to take the College Board documentation of their accommodations with them to the testing center. Some AP teachers send a letter home to remind parents of the location of the testing center, the exam time, and what the student should bring. If this is your practice, please make sure to include a note about accommodations documentation for the parents of students with disabilities. Please see Figure 7.2 for a resource for students taking the AP exam.

FIGURE 7.2. RESOURCE

There is a series of books titled *5 Steps to a 5* available in local bookstores and online that provides test preparation and review for AP exams by content area. If you do not already have students use these books, please review them.

International Baccalaureate (IB)

The IB has a range of three programs (Primary Years, Middle Years, and Diploma) in 141 countries, including the United States (IB 2011a). The United States has more than 1,300 schools with 782 Diploma programs. The purpose of the IB programs is to promote high-quality global education. Recently, the IB has committed to serving students with disabilities and recognizing individual learner needs.

The IB schedules exams for May and November. The exact dates of the exams will vary from year to year. If you are an IB teacher, you will know the schedule for your students. The IB offers both IB schools and programs within a school. The IB schools require an application for admission, in which case most of the required documentation will be part of the student's application file. You will just need to confirm what the accommodations are by contacting the school's IB assessment coordinator. If you are a science teacher in an IB program that is not in an IB school, you will need to have your school's IB coordinator contact the IB Curriculum and Assessment office for your region to determine the necessary steps to be taken.

The IB has established guidelines for allowable student accommodations in a policy handbook. Your school's coordinator will have access to this document. Generally, these guidelines allow for flexibility to help foster a more inclusive community (IB 2011b). Once a student with a disability is placed in your IB science classroom, please contact your school's coordinator to review the accommodations guidelines. At this time, you may also want to discuss a plan to ensure that the student has the necessary support to be successful in the end-of-year tests. Please see Figure 7.3 for a website resource on IB and assessment of students with special needs.

FIGURE 7.3. CONTACT INFORMATION FOR IB PROGRAMS

The International Baccalaureate (IB) programs provide an Online Curriculum Center (OCC) for participating schools that includes information for students with disabilities. The website for the OCC is located at *http://occ.ibo.org/ibis/occ/guest/home.cfm.* Please note that you will need your school login and password to access these resources. Please check with your school's IB coordinator.

Working With Students and Parents

As part of the IEP team, parents should be in the loop for any communication regarding testing accommodations. Sometimes parents will independently hire a psychologist to provide eligibility testing and documentation to request testing accommodations. In these cases, someone on the IEP team (such as a special education teacher or guidance counselor) should regularly communicate with the parents to ensure deadlines are met.

It may be appropriate for some students to take responsibility for ensuring that the testing accommodations are requested from the College Board or IB. The importance of students learning to self-advocate has been previously discussed. Requesting her own accommodations encourages the student to self-advocate in a meaningful way and provides good practice for when she is in college. See "Fostering Student Independence" for questions students should ask themselves when self-advocating for their examination experience. Again, a student's ability to manage this type of request and process needs to be an IEP team discussion, but it is always good to consider ways in which students can become more responsible for his own education.

FOSTERING STUDENT INDEPENDENCE

Student, ask yourself the following questions:

- Have I reviewed my transition plan? Do I know the steps I'm supposed to take?
- When is the deadline for registering for the exam? What do I need to turn in to register by the deadline?
- Who is making sure I get my accommodations requested?
- Do I have a plan for review of the material before the test?
- When is the test?
- Where is the testing center?
- What should I bring with me?

Calendar

The following is a recommended planning outline for helping assist students to obtain and use any needed testing accommodations for the end-of-year tests. Remember that all of your students will take these tests, so test preparation is important for the entire class. Planning is essential for success!

August Through September

Once you have identified any students with 504 plans or IEPs in your class, you should plan to review the accommodations pages for each student. Please make a note of students who may need testing accommodations. You will also want to identify the case manager or guidance counselor who is assigned to the student. Please review the transition plan and note if there is a person (including the student) designated to request testing accommodations from the College Board or IB.

Please plan to have an initial meeting with any students with disabilities (and the special education teacher) to discuss your expectations for the class. This is a good time to have students sign a learning contract and review the safety contract. Please see Chapter 5 (p. 74) for an example of a safety contract and Figure 7.4 (p. 112) for an example of a learning contract. Please plan to take the following steps:

- Identify students with 504 plans or IEPs.
- Review the 504 plan or IEP, noting accommodations.
- Contact the student's case manager or guidance counselor.
- Establish who will be responsible for requesting testing accommodations from the appropriate third party.

October Through December

Plan to build test-taking skills into your instruction. Please read Chapter 4 (Figure 4.9 [p. 66]) for suggestions on how to incorporate these skills into your instruction. Sometimes a student will need to have further psychological testing to document the need for testing accommodations. Because scheduling these types of appointments can be time consuming, ongoing communication with the students' parents and IEP team will be required to meet any deadlines for submitting the request to the College Board or IB. Please note that some IB examinations are in November, so plan to know the schedule if you are an IB teacher. Please plan to do the following:

- Incorporate practice test questions into instruction.
- Maintain communication with parents, the guidance counselor, and the IEP team.
- Know the deadline for requesting testing accommodations. (This will change yearly.)
- If you are an IB teacher, please know the exam schedule.

January Through March

Continue to work on test preparation with all of your students. Monitor students with disabilities to ensure that they are using their test accommodations during practice tests. If they are not using their accommodations, please contact the special education teacher for assistance. For students who need outside testing to document their need for accommodations, please note that this testing should be scheduled early in the year. You probably already noted the date, time, and place that the actual exam is scheduled, but you want to make sure you have this information easily available for any communication with the IEP team or parents. Please plan to do the following:

- Continue test preparation.
- Communicate with students, parents, and the IEP team regarding test date, time, and place.
- Verify that testing accommodations have been requested for the student.

April

This is the time to begin final test preparation for all of your students. You may discuss relaxation techniques to alleviate test anxiety, remind students what materials they should bring to the testing center, and conduct practice tests. Students who have testing accommodations should be reminded to use them during the actual exam. Please plan to do the following:

- Continue to prepare students to take the exam.
- Follow up as needed with the student, parents, and IEP team.

May

The College Board's AP and IB tests are administered this month. You may want to remind students about the date, time, and place and any materials that they are allowed to bring to the exam. Please plan to do the following:

- Remind students of the date, time, and location of the testing center.
- Remind students to take any needed testing documentation with them.
- Ensure students can use any online submission or testing procedures.

June Through July

As you know, test results are scored and reported during these months. Prior to the end of school, you may want to remind students that score reports will be mailed to the address given when they registered for the exam. Additionally, you may want to solicit feedback from students about how they felt using their testing accommodations. For example, did the accommodation work for the student? How did they feel about their test performance? This feedback will provide insight into how students with disabilities are using their accommodations and how you can better prepare them in the future. Please plan to do the following:

- Reflect on your test preparation instruction. For example, what worked? What content do you need to spend more time on? Do you need to make any changes?
- Consider the students with disabilities' feedback on their accommodations. Is there anything you need to consider for next year?
- Reflect on your communication with the parents and the IEP team. What could you do better next year? Do you need to follow up?

FIGURE 7.4. LEARNING CONTRACT EXAMPLE

Student: ______________________ **Teacher:** ______________________

Class and content: *Example*: Advanced Placement (AP) Chemistry
Please note that you are responsible for reading the course syllabus on your own.
____

Date contract begins:______________________

Student and teacher agree to the following (student and teacher should negotiate):

1. Student will come to class prepared. This includes completing reading assignments and bringing textbook, notebook, paper and pencil, graphing calculator, and other materials.

Notes:

2. Student will complete a reduced number of homework problems. The number of assigned homework problems will vary depending on the content of the assignment and will be at the teacher's discretion.

Notes:

3. Student will use the accommodations stated on the IEP. This includes extended time for tests, advanced notes pages, and assigned seating.

Notes:

4. Student will request testing accommodations for the end-of-year AP test from the College Board. The school guidance counselor will assist in this request. Student will use the testing accommodations.

Notes:

Student signature: ______________________________

Teacher signature: ______________________________

Parent signature: ______________________________

Conclusion

This chapter addressed requesting testing accommodations for students who need them from either the College Board or IB. You are already aware of the testing procedures used for AP and IB tests, so it is just a matter of determining who needs testing accommodations, who is responsible for requesting them, and what deadlines are involved. While the process of requesting accommodations and working with an IEP team may seem daunting at first, it will become much easier with experience.

Remember that planning is essential to success! Please make sure to begin identifying which students will need to have testing accommodations requested before the school year begins, then plan to follow up to ensure that all of the deadlines are met. The IEP team and the student can help you manage this process and ensure success for the student.

IDEAS TO GET YOU STARTED

- Identify students who need testing accommodations.
- Determine who will be responsible (e.g., student, guidance counselor) for submitting the request to the testing agency (AP or IB).
- Know the testing schedule from the AP or IB.
- Know students' accommodations and encourage their use.
- Incorporate test-taking skill development into your instruction.

References

College Board. 2011. Annual AP program participation report. *http://professionals.collegeboard.com/profdownload/AP-Annual-Participation.pdf*

College Board. 2012. Services for students with disabilities. *www.collegeboard.com/ssd/student/index.html*

International Baccalaureate. 2011a. IB fast facts. *www.ibo.org/facts/fastfacts/index.cfm*

International Baccalaureate. 2011b. Information for educators. *www.ibo.org/informationfor/educators/coordinators/index.cfm*

CHAPTER 8

Final Thoughts

Most students, including those with disabilities, in advanced classes are highly motivated to succeed academically. As educational policymakers have looked toward increasing Advanced Placement (AP), International Baccalaureat (IB), and honors classes as a way to foster more intellectually rigorous academic experiences, they have noted that students in these classes have high personal aspirations (Bleske-Resech, Lubinski, and Benbow 2004). Though Bleske-Resech, Lubinski, and Benbow's study centered on students who are "intellectually precocious" (2004, p. 217), this speaks to the population taking AP courses and would include academically advanced students with disabilities as well as students without disabilities. As early as 1964, Frankel noted that students enrolled in an Advanced Studies summer study program increased their self-concepts in the areas of self-reliance and special talents (Frankel 1964). Subsequent studies have also shown that students in AP and IB courses are more satisfied with their intellectual experience in high school classes and pursued higher education at greater rates than their peers who did not take AP or IB courses (Bleske-Resech, Lubinski, and Benbow 2004).

In fact, advanced classes are seen as places to recruit students into college science, technology, engineering, and mathematics (STEM) classes (NRC 2002). With the increased focus on encouraging women, minorities, and people with disabilities to enter STEM fields, it is likely that more and more students with disabilities will be taking your advanced classes. This does not mean the curriculum and high standards of your classes should change!

Not all students can succeed in the advanced science classroom, but for many students, the skills learned in these classes are important to later success in college. As a science teacher, you have a vital role to play in the development of potential scientists, researchers, science teachers, and educated citizens. Your lessons help students learn how to hypothesize, collect and analyze data, draw conclusions based on facts, and develop skills for managing college coursework.

Previous chapters have discussed the many different aspects of including students with disabilities in these advanced classes. However, one of the most important foundations for student success is you. Particularly important are your openness and willingness to welcome students with disabilities into your classroom. So, the following discussion will address concerns related to recruiting students with disabilities into an advanced classroom, participating in coteaching, and working with students with disabilities as a way to foster your own growth as a teacher.

Recruitment

As discussed throughout this book, students with disabilities should only be placed in your class if they have the ability to succeed. However, a disability should not become a limitation for these students. Students with disabilities often are seen as less capable than their nondisabled peers. In many ways, this perception can be more disabling than the actual disability because it limits students' aspirations and dreams for the future.

Students are recruited into advanced classes in different ways, depending on the school and district policies. Sometimes any student who tests at a minimum aptitude will be offered advanced coursework, while some schools rely exclusively on teacher recommendations. Most schools use a combination of grades, test scores, and teacher recommendations. For students with disabilities, the IEP team will often pursue placement in an advanced class for a student. In some cases, the parent may make the request for the student to take one of these classes. However, for many students, including those with disabilities, a personal connection with a science teacher is critical to the decision to attempt advanced coursework.

Simply, a student may have taken a previous science class with you and enjoyed the experience. Or you may have realized that a particular student seems to have an interest and ability in a science topic. You encourage him or her to take an advanced class. Your belief that students can achieve at the highest levels in science can instill confidence and encourage them to reach higher.

This is especially true for students with disabilities. Please think about students with disabilities in your other science classes. Could they do the work in your advanced classes? Sometimes the disability may "mask" their actual abilities in science. The student may appear too disorganized for advanced coursework, but may have aptitude for scientific inquiry. You could speak with the special education teacher to discuss the possibilities of support in your advanced class. Often just letting the student know that you think he has the potential to take your advanced class may motivate him to work harder in the current science class. This can be life changing for any student: a teacher who believes in her and helps her consider future possibilities!

Please set high standards for all of your students and recruit students with disabilities into your advanced classes. They can also benefit from the intellectual challenges and confidence that come from pursuing advanced coursework. Encourage students with disabilities in your classes to pursue advanced coursework just as you would encourage any potential science student. It can make a difference in their futures. Who knows—one of these students could become the next Stephen Hawking, Albert Einstein, or Marie Curie. Please see Figure 8.1 for some benefits of enrolling in these classes.

FIGURE 8.1. ADVANCED COURSEWORK: STUDENT BENEFITS

- More prepared for college coursework
    - o Consider study skills such as note-taking and homework completion.
    - o Consider test-taking skills.
    - o Consider organizational and time-management skills, such as the ability to manage multiple homework assignments and due dates.
- More likely to graduate college
- More confident in their academic abilities and special talents
- More self-reliant
    - o Consider the suggestions in the Fostering Student Independence boxes throughout this book.
    - o Consider independent research projects that students conduct in your class.

Sources: Bleske-Resech, Lubinski, and Benbow 2004; Frankel 1964.

Co-Teaching

In the past few years, more general education classes are being co-taught, which means that a science teacher and a special education teacher share a classroom and teach together (Friend and Cook 2009). You may even co-teach or team teach your science classes, though it is rare to team teach an advanced class. However, as more students with disabilities take advanced coursework, you may want to consider team teaching with a special education teacher in these classes.

If you are currently team teaching a science class, then you realize the benefits of having two teachers in the classroom, such as for monitoring students during labs, sharing the homework grading, and taking turns during instruction (Linz, Heater, and Howard 2011). If you have not team taught a science class, then you might want to consider the possibilities of teaming. This can be a terrific way to support students with disabilities in any of your classes, as special education teachers may have suggestions on how to incorporate student accommodations, differentiate instruction, and communicate with parents.

While a special education teacher may not be knowledgeable about advanced science content, they are very knowledgeable about special education and how to assist students with disabilities. You may want to explore teaming up for your advanced class with a special education teacher. The special education teacher may be very receptive to teaching with you and open to learning more about science. Once you have decided to team with a special education teacher in your advanced class, both of you may want to approach your school administration to request a teaming assignment.

It can take time to build a relationship with your co-teacher as you both must learn the best way to communicate, recognize that each person has pet peeves, and teach together. Your administrator can be most helpful by adjusting the master schedule to allow you and your teaching partner (special education teacher) time together to plan. In fact, one of the biggest factors in successful co-teaching is common planning time (Scruggs, Mastropieri, and McDuffie 2007).

Co-planning time allows both teachers to address issues and concerns in their classrooms. When co-teaching, it is best to think of a classroom and students as "our classroom" or "our students." It can be hard making the transition from "my classroom" to "our classroom," but it helps to have everyone focus on the team aspect of co-teaching (Potts and Howard 2011). In some team-taught classes, it can be difficult to distinguish who is the content-area teacher and who is the special education teacher. However, due to the advanced science content in your class, it will be apparent that you are the science teacher. Should you attempt team teaching in your advanced science classes, please strive to include the special education teacher as your equal partner. While you are the expert on science content, he can make contributions to the instruction of the class. He can learn the advanced science content with a little time and help from you and also recommend strategies regardless of the depth of his understanding of the content.

During your co-planning time, both teachers need to discuss grading, logistics, IEP goals, needed accommodations, and any other issue that may arise in your classroom (Howard and Potts 2009). This can also be an opportunity to review how specific students are managing in the advanced class. You may already have a team-taught class and co-planning time for other science classes you teach. You may recognize how this time is invaluable for problem solving with your teaching partner. Please see Figure 8.2 for a co-planning checklist that can help ensure you and your partner cover the important items during planning time.

Team teaching is becoming more common, and you may already have experience with a teaching partner. Many schools offer in-service trainings, time to observe

FIGURE 8.2. CO-TEACHING PLANNING CHECKLIST

Standards

Did we do the following tasks?

- ☐ Use the standards as the focal point of the lesson
- ☐ Include opportunities to connect to IEP goals

Accommodations and Modifications

Did we accomplish these items?

- ☐ Address any non-content-related goals
- ☐ Address appropriate content-related IEP goals
- ☐ Consider needs of individual students for assignments and classwork
- ☐ Discuss how to provide appropriate accommodations and modifications without alienating students with disabilities?

Assessment

Did we take the following actions?

- ☐ Start with the end in mind
- ☐ Include formative assessment
- ☐ Include summative assessment
- ☐ Assess in a variety of formats
    - ☐ Paper and pencil
    - ☐ Project-based
    - ☐ Oral
    - ☐ Presentations

- ☐ Agree on grading procedures
    - ☐ Who is responsible
    - ☐ Differentiating grading based on student needs
    - ☐ Use of rubrics

- ☐ Talk about homework
    - ☐ How much to assign
    - ☐ How often to assign
    - ☐ How to grade
    - ☐ Accepting late work
    - ☐ Procedures for turning in homework

Instructional Strategies

Did we consider including any of the following methods?

- ☐ Mnemonics
- ☐ Graphic organizers
- ☐ Cooperative learning strategies
- ☐ Progress monitoring
- ☐ Peer-assisted learning strategies

Logistics

Who will prepare the following?

- ☐ Materials
- ☐ Tests

Did we plan for the following issues?

- ☐ Roles in instruction
- ☐ Roles in discipline
- ☐ Classroom movement patterns

Source: Howard and Potts 2009. Used with permission.

other co-teaching teams, and materials on co-teaching. You may want to contact your administrator or special education department to identify what resources are available in your school. We encourage you to consider the possibility of team teaching your advanced classes as a way to include students with disabilities.

Conclusion

Finally, one of the most rewarding aspects of including students with disabilities in your advanced class is the opportunity to enhance your own individual teaching skills. Having a student with a disability in our classroom often encourages us to think about new ways to present material or redesign an experiment. This can lead to new insights and ways of doing things, as well as better outcomes for all of our students.

You will also have the opportunity to learn more about special education laws and perspectives, as well as how to assist students with disabilities. You may get to try out new technologies and use current technologies in new ways. There are many professional development opportunities available for assisting science teachers to teach students with disabilities. Please explore the resources discussed in this book. You may even find new resources that can help you.

It can also regenerate our passion for teaching. We can learn from all of our students, including those with disabilities. Sometimes the lesson may be as simple as being persistent in setting up an experiment or a profound insight into our own humanity. Of course, not every lesson in your science classroom is going to lead to a teaching "breakthrough," but there is the possibility and that can be very rewarding. Most teachers want to make a difference in the lives of their students. By including students with disabilities in your advanced science classes, you can help the student achieve her potential and your other students to be more accept-

IDEAS TO GET YOU STARTED

- Review the ideas in previous chapters.
- Get to know the special education teachers at your school.
- Recruit students with disabilities into your advanced classes.
- Consider how you can inspire students with disabilities to work toward their highest potential.
- Explore the life histories of scientists with disabilities.

ing of differences. These are important lessons that you can teach just as you teach advanced scientific principles

References

Bleske-Resech, A., D. Lubinski, and C. P. Benbow. 2004. Meeting the educational needs of special populations: Advanced placement's role in developing exceptional human capital. *Psychological Science* 15 (4): 217–224.

Frankel, E. 1964. Effects of a program of advanced summer study on the self-perceptions of academically talented high school students. *Exceptional Children* 30 (6): 245–249.

Friend, M., and L. Cook. 2009. *Interactions: Collaboration skills for school professionals.* 6th ed. New York: Pearson Education.

Howard, L., and E. A. Potts. 2009. Using co-planning time: Strategies for a successful co-teaching marriage. *TEACHING Exceptional Children Plus* 5 (4). *http://escholarship.bc.edu/education/tecplus/vol5/iss2/art2*

Linz, E., M. J. Heater, and L. A. Howard. 2011. *Team teaching science: Success for all learners*. Arlington, VA: National Science Teachers Association.

National Research Council (NRC). 2002. *Learning and understanding: Improving advanced study of mathematics and science in U.S. high schools.* Committee on Programs for Advanced Study of Mathematics and Science in American High Schools. J. P. Gollub, M. W. Bertenthal, J. B. Labov, and P. C. Curtis, eds. Center for Education. Division of Behavioral and Social Science and Education. Washington, DC: National Academies Press.

Potts, E. A., and L. A. Howard. 2011. *How to co-teach: A guide for general and special educators.* Baltimore, MD: Brookes Publishing.

Scruggs, T. E., M. A. Mastropieri, and K. A. McDuffie. 2007. Co-teaching in inclusive classrooms: A metasynthesis of qualitative research. *Exceptional Children* 73 (4): 392–416.

INDEX

Page numbers printed in ***boldface*** type refer to figures and tables.

INDEX

INDEX

INDEX

INDEX

INDEX

INDEX

INDEX

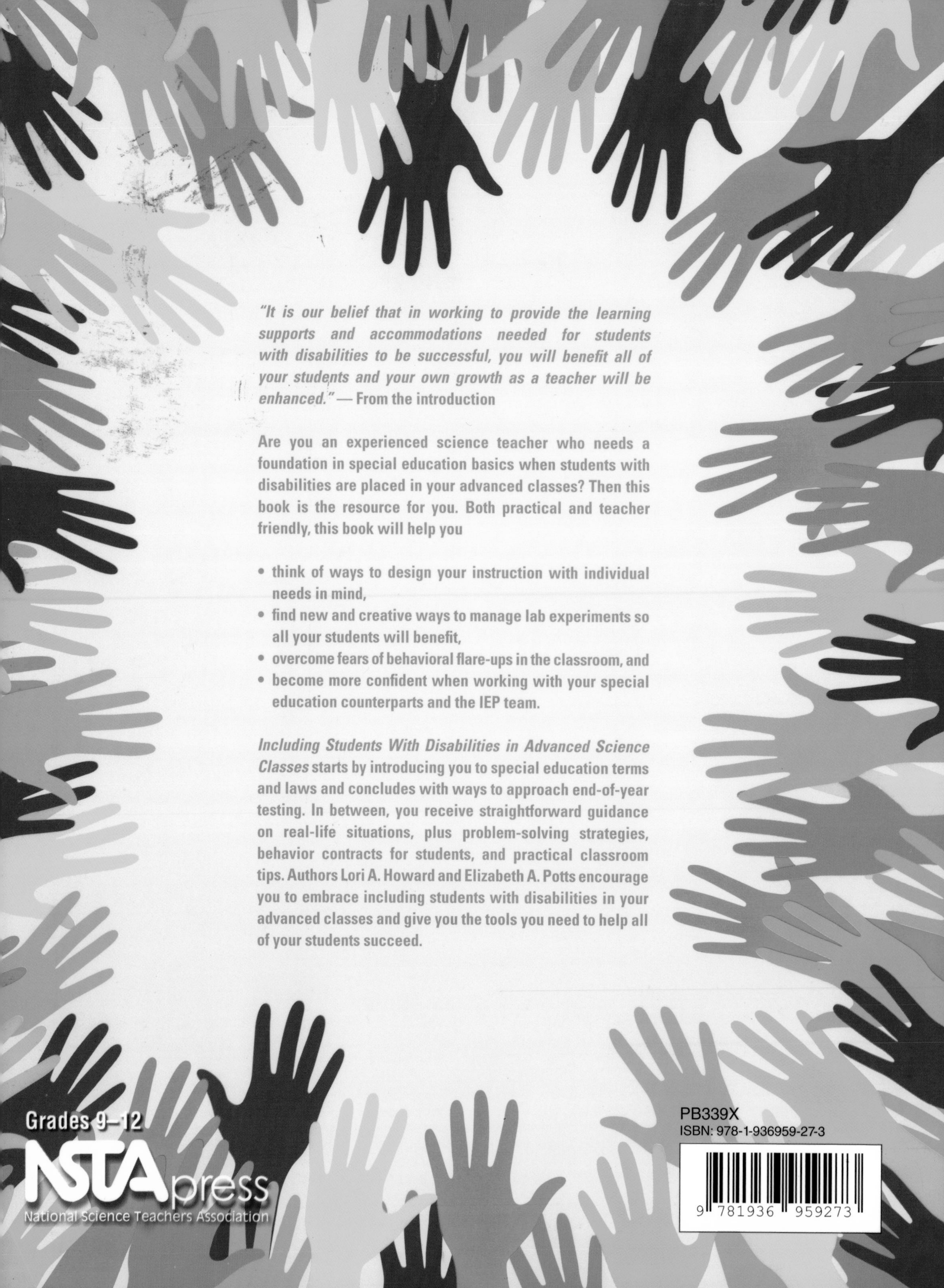

"It is our belief that in working to provide the learning supports and accommodations needed for students with disabilities to be successful, you will benefit all of your students and your own growth as a teacher will be enhanced." — From the introduction

Are you an experienced science teacher who needs a foundation in special education basics when students with disabilities are placed in your advanced classes? Then this book is the resource for you. Both practical and teacher friendly, this book will help you

- think of ways to design your instruction with individual needs in mind,
- find new and creative ways to manage lab experiments so all your students will benefit,
- overcome fears of behavioral flare-ups in the classroom, and
- become more confident when working with your special education counterparts and the IEP team.

Including Students With Disabilities in Advanced Science Classes starts by introducing you to special education terms and laws and concludes with ways to approach end-of-year testing. In between, you receive straightforward guidance on real-life situations, plus problem-solving strategies, behavior contracts for students, and practical classroom tips. Authors Lori A. Howard and Elizabeth A. Potts encourage you to embrace including students with disabilities in your advanced classes and give you the tools you need to help all of your students succeed.

Grades 9–12

NSTA press
National Science Teachers Association

PB339X
ISBN: 978-1-936959-27-3

9 781936 959273